# DECISION MAKING ESSENTIALS

## YOU ALWAYS WANTED TO KNOW

**MARK KOSCINSKI**

**VIBRANT**
PUBLISHERS

# Decision Making Essentials

## You Always Wanted To Know

Paperback ISBN 10: 1-63651-002-7
Paperback ISBN 13: 978-1-63651-002-6

Ebook ISBN 10: 1-63651-003-5
Ebook ISBN 13: 978-1-63651-003-3

Hardback ISBN 10: 1-63651-004-3
Hardback ISBN 13: 978-1-63651-004-0

Library of Congress Control Number: 2020945968

Vibrant Publishers books are available at special quantity discount for sales promotions, or for use in corporate training programs. For more information please write to bulkorders@vibrantpublishers.com

Please email feedback / corrections (technical, grammatical or spelling) to spellerrors@vibrantpublishers.com

To access the complete catalogue of Vibrant Publishers, visit www.vibrantpublishers.com

# BUY 3 FOR THE PRICE OF 2

## USE DISCOUNT CODE 3FOR2

*Discount applies to the lowest value item.

Cannot be combined with other offers | Offer valid till stocks last | Offer valid only on

## www.vibrantpublishers.com

*This page is intentionally left blank*

# What experts say about this book!

*This is the first book that I've read that details decision-making with such depth. Mark Koscinki is able to take seemingly complicated information and break it down into short, easy-to-understand chapters, summarize the key points, and offer questions to ensure one's understanding of decision-making processes. I recommend it to those in leadership and to those aspiring to leadership roles!*

**– Jacqueline Childress, J.D.**
**Adjunct Associate Professor at Austin Community College**

*In this unparalleled textbook, Mark Koscinski has done an excellent job providing the relevant keys to effective decision-making. By providing the necessary details of transforming decision-making into success, Mark Koscinski takes the simple art of choosing into a science that allows managers to consistently make those choices that benefit the workplace.*

**– Sonja B. Wilson, PhD**
**President at Wilson's Professional Training Services, Inc.**

*An exemplary, masterfully-written, comprehensive guide into the navigation of the management realm. I admire the author's adeptness at framing the content by incorporating topics relating to management, accounting, economics, and statistics—a holistic approach to decision making.*

**– Dr. Dawn A. Humburg CPA PhD**
**Professor at Iowa Central Community College**

# What experts say about this book!

*As a college professor I am constantly looking for ways to incorporate decision making skills into my classes and this is the perfect book. My students are provided with a flexible system that makes sense in today's world. My students will be able to learn how to make decisions based on the theory we are learning!*

**– Heather Nestorick,**

**Accounting Professor at Luzerne County Community College**

*The greatest threat to my business success and survival in the early years was the quality of my decision making. I did not know what I did not know and that made solid decision making risky. Every poor decision provided a lesson to learn and the motivation not to make the same mistake twice. As the business grew so grew the significance of the decisions. I never tire of learning new decision making models, practicing my decision making and helping others to learn as well. Decision Making Essentials is a great way to refresh my skillfulness and develop those around me. Being a strong process decision maker has contributed to my consulting effectiveness and value-added to my client relationships.*

**– Leslie Yerkes**

**Founder**

**Catalyst Consulting Group, Inc.**

# What experts say about this book!

*I think the book is a great addition to the Management Series. The author has included numerous examples to illustrate the concept which makes it easier to understand and follow. Some of the chapters seem to be a bit technical but overall the book is quite helpful for a beginner or businessman to successfully accomplish his decision making responsibilities.*

**– Tony Ruscitto**

**Professor at New York University & Touro College**

**Corporate Director of Human Resources**

**Fitzpatrick Hotel Group, North America**

# About the Author

Mark Koscinski, a certified public accountant, is an assistant professor of accounting practice at Moravian College in Bethlehem, Pennsylvania. He teaches undergraduate courses in accounting and decision analysis on a graduate level. Mark has over forty years of experience in the corporate and not-for-profit worlds. He served as chief financial officer and corporate controller of companies in the toy, banking, investment banking and defense contracting industries. He holds a B.A. in economics with high honors and an M.B.A in professional accounting from Rutgers University in New Jersey. He earned a doctorate from Drew University, in New Jersey as well. His research interests lie in artificial intelligence, machine learning, and decision analysis, as they apply to the sports world. Mark is happily married to his wife Susan and has three children and four grandchildren.

# Preface

My lovely wife Susan told me about a manager who had difficulty making a decision. She asked if I could create a one-page decision tree outlining the decision making process for this manager. I politely declined and said I would have to write a book to cover the topic. I did, and this is the book.

Decision analysis is leaping forward every year with new developments. Artificial intelligence, behavioral economics, machine learning, big data, data science and other developments make this a wonderful and very fertile field of study. Despite the flurry of activity, there doesn't seem to be a handbook for decision-makers. Many of the books talk about decision making methodologies in great detail, but don't really address the peripheral issues such as ethics, morality, time horizons, etc. It seems as if the decision is made in a timeless and static environment, not subject to internal control process, project planning, and management review. This book is a modest attempt to address these issues.

I would like to dedicate this book to my colleagues at Moravian College. It is a wonderful place to explore your intellectual curiosity and teach. Of course, I also dedicate it to my wife Susan, a kind and gentle soul and a dedicated health care professional. Without her help, I couldn't have even attempted or have been motivated to write this book.

*This page is intentionally left blank*

# Table of Contents

*This page is intentionally left blank*

# Chapter **1**

# Introduction to Decision Making

This chapter explores the characteristics of decision making and the definition of decision analysis. Some of the key issues and pitfalls in decision making such as framing are also discussed.

You are taking the vacation of a lifetime when a major catastrophe strikes the cruise ship. The rest of the passengers and you make it safely to the lifeboats as you watch the crippled ship slip beneath the ocean. You are days from any port, and you know the ship sank so fast no Mayday warning could possibly have been broadcast. Another horrible realization soon sets in. There are nine passengers in a lifeboat built to hold six. The lifeboat is becoming unstable because of the extra weight and is in danger of sinking too. What do you and the other passengers do?

By this time, you surely recognize this as the famous lifeboat problem. It is usually supplemented with the background information about: who is on the boat, what are their professions, if they have children etc. The following question is posed to the readers: who should remain in the lifeboat? The readers will pour over that information, making moral value judgments on who will survive and who will be forced overboard.

The lifeboat problem illustrates a particular problem in decision analysis called **framing**. The way a question is posed sometimes dictates the answer. The readers draw the inference three of the passengers must be consigned to their demise. Very few readers will come up with a seemingly obvious answer: healthy passengers can take turns in the water holding onto the lifeboat for a time. They can return to the lifeboat for rest while other passengers take their place in the water. The way the question was framed helped dictate the solutions the students proposed. Reframing a question is often necessary to see if the potential solution set was restricted by the how the question was framed. Perhaps better solutions were eliminated by the framing and not fully considered. Framing in decision making is just one of the difficulties we will examine in this book.

Isaac Asimov, a famous and prolific author on many subjects, wrote a science fiction story almost sixty years ago called The Machine That Won the War. It is widely available and is a very short read. In the distant future, the human race just won a war against an alien race called the Denebians.[1] Earth's military strategy was dictated by an advanced computer named Multivac.[2] Three key officials of the government gather to talk about the victory. Henderson, the programmer of Multivac sheepishly admits he altered the data fed to Multivac since he didn't trust the information. This seems to have gone well beyond the typical data

---

1. For the scientifically minded, the star Deneb is in the constellation Cygnus and is over 800 parsecs from earth.

2. Asimov wrote several Multivac short stories. All are still worth reading and, in many ways, presaged artificial intelligence.

scrubbing and transformation data scientists do today. Jablonsky, the operator of Multivac then admits he altered the output from Multivac since he knew it was not functioning properly. Finally, Swift, the Executive Director of the government, admits he didn't rely on Multivac at all and made the decisions using another method. When pressed, Swift produced a coin and asked, heads or tails?

This short impactful story reveals many truths about decision making. Poor data can result in poor decisions. A poor decision model–in this case–an artificial intelligence not kept updated or in full repair-- can result in erroneous recommendations and decisions. Another is a decision-maker can often ignore the recommendations of the decision model (or experts) and reach another conclusion if the data, methodology and **decision rule** are considered faulty.

Swift, the final authority as executive director, ignored the recommendation of Multivac and relied on pure chance to make the decision. Even a faulty method such as flipping a coin can sometimes result in a good decision!

Decisions are made every day in organizations. These decisions range from major, strategic decisions such as articulating the organization's mission and value proposition to small decisions such as who can park in the reserved lot and who will receive the corner office.

Decisions usually involve some or all of the following characteristics:

1. **Risk**[3] and/or **uncertainty**;

2. One or more decision **attributes**;

3. One or more **objectives**; and

4. One or more interested **stakeholders**.

An **objective** is the goal or target of the decision. It implies a direction and desired movement towards the objective. An attribute is a factor or element considered in making the decision. The greater the number of attributes, objectives, and stakeholders, the more complex the decision process and the greater the difficulty in arriving at a final decision.

The decision-maker can be a single individual for smaller decisions, or a group such as a committee or a board of directors for more important decisions. In this book the term "decision-maker" will include both individual and group decision-makers.

We would like to believe all decisions are made rationally. Put it another way, if a decision-maker is prepared to accept a rational decision-rule, the outcome of the decision analysis should be chosen. As we will see, completely rational decision making is not entirely the reality of the situation. The human mind can only efficiently process so much information. This problem is compounded by our limited memories as well. Often times bias will sneak into our decision making. Our analysis will often conflict with our intuitive approach to making a decision. Quick, intuitive decisions are often wrong. How decision-makers make decisions with limited processing ability is one topic of this book.

---

3. Highlighted words are included in the Glossary.

Mythology teaches us a silver bullet can destroy all supernatural creatures such as vampires and werewolves. In our modern culture, the phrase silver bullet has come to mean a universal solution to any problem. Alas, there is no silver bullet in decision analysis. There isn't one decision making model to fit all situations. Situational factors are often key in determining what decision analysis model to use. For example, financial decisions need to be supported by financial analysis. Personnel decisions often depend on other, less quantifiable attributes.[4]

One commonality to all types of decision making is analysis. Some form of analysis must be done to make the best decision possible. The field of **decision analysis** could be thought of as a toolbox containing a variety of methodologies. These tools help the decision-maker assign probabilities to potential outcomes and make the decision process explicit. As there is no certainty in the business world, the decision-maker can often only "play the odds" and choose the option to provide the best chance of success. Explicitly stating the analysis will allow other stakeholders to critique the methodology and its results, hopefully adding to its reliability. This book will provide you with a toolbox of insights you can open and use whenever you are dealing with a difficult problem.

We begin our journey with a simple decision model. Making a major decision requires a structured approach. The decision-maker first needs to frame and pose the question. Then gather data and analyze their findings. The decision-maker then applies a decision rule or a way to make a judgement between competing alternatives to arrive at a proposed solution.

---

4. Although time precludes further discussion, the use of an algorithm or a checklist to make hiring decisions often leads to superior hiring results.

An explanation and negotiation phase may be needed when the decision - maker attempts to gain "buy in" from superiors, colleagues, subordinates and other stakeholders. The decision-maker may have to negotiate an agreement both outside and inside the organization. Decision analysis tools can be helpful here too. Even after the decision-maker "sells" his decision, implementation can be a major headache. Ask anyone who has implemented a major change in software such as migrating to an Enterprise Resource System. A post-implementation review of the decision and its execution should also be undertaken.

In summary, this book is aimed at decision-makers across all organizations and operations. It takes a commonsense approach to the decision making process as it examines some key principles of decision analysis.

# Chapter Summary

◆ Framing a question in a particular way might affect the outcome of a decision.

◆ The decision making process is fraught with potential problems including the limited cognitive processing ability of the decision-maker, limited memory, and poor information.

◆ Decision analysis does not provide the answer to your question. It provides input for your decision. Nevertheless, this input should improve the quality of the decision being made.

◆ There isn't a single method of decision analysis fitting all circumstances. We do best to think about the field of decision analysis as providing a toolbox of methodologies for decision-makers as they approach problems.

◆ A decision rule is a way to make judgments between competing alternatives.

# Discussion Questions

1. Read the short story The Machine That Won the War by Isaac Asimov. Approach this from a systems perspective. What went wrong? How could each issue have been corrected?

2. In 1884, four sailors were afloat in a lifeboat at sea. They rapidly ran out of provisions. One of the sailors killed the youngest member of the four and the remaining three resorted to cannibalism to survive. The three were eventually rescued. Evaluate their decision.

3. One problem often encountered in decision making is a lack of information. Can you have too much data when making a decision?

---

*Solutions to the above questions can be downloaded from the* **Online Resources** *section of this book on* **www.vibrantpublishers.com**

---

# Chapter 2

## Cognitive Processes and Their Limitations

> Classical economics asserts we are rational decision-makers. This chapter explores why we may not be because of our biases and cognitive processing issues. Behavioral economics, including prospect theory, is also discussed.

## 2.1 Introduction

Professional theologians coined the term **hermeneutic insight**. In its simplest form, this theory of textual interpretation states anyone reading a sacred scripture will interpret the whole of the document by reference to certain parts of it. The overall understanding of the document will depend on each reader's understanding of the passages selected. This has been labeled as the "canon within the canon" problem, or the emphasizing of certain parts of the scripture and the deemphasizing or total exclusion of other parts. As one of my professors once put it, "everyone brings their own baggage to scripture." The economics profession did not come to widely understand or appreciate this insight until the later part of the twentieth century.

We would all like to believe we make decisions in a completely rational manner. Economic theory assumes this is the case, giving rise to the image of the **economic man**[5]: a person who makes decisions rationally and with perfect information in order to satisfy his or her utility function. As we will see, it may not be practical, desirable or even possible to fulfill the perfect information requirement. Many decisions are made under conditions of uncertainty, a condition we will turn to in later chapters.

The fields of **behavioral finance, behavioral economics** and psychology have challenged the assumption of the economic man. As it turns out, decision making processes are much more complex than the simple calculus of economics supposes. Classical economics was criticized for assuming the maximization of profit was the same as maximizing utility. It also does not leave room for cognitive biases and limitations in the decision making process. This chapter explores some of the interesting cognitive processes we employ when we are making decisions, the biases we possess, and the limitations of our cognitive processes.

Before we begin though, it is also important to note these fields of study are not without their critics. The best term to describe what many minimizers of the study of the behavioral scientists believe is the entire field is relatively unstructured. Any deviation from the result predicted by classical economics can be ascribed to one or more of the phenomena described in this chapter or in other studies after the fact. The various behavioral theories described in this chapter read like a laundry list of cognitive

---

5. Called "Econs" by the psychology profession.

processing errors, but they may not accurately predict how someone comes to choose any one particular option. Critics ask for a behavioral theory that is predictive.[6] They ask for a unified theory that can explain the entire range of phenomena. These commentators deny the behavioral disciplines provide a refutation of the classical economic model. In the field of behavioral finance, **Eugene Fama (b. 1939)**, a Nobel Prize winning economist notes the behavioral schools are not consistent in explaining the reasons why decisions may vary from classical economics. In some studies deviations are cited as both overreactions and as underreactions to market forces.

The behavioral schools make many valid points about decision making but the extent these factors impact decisions is still controversial. While it is difficult if not impossible to eradicate all bias and cognitive processing limitations from any one individual, organizations understand this as they require major decisions to be vetted by either a committee of decision-makers or senior management. Major decisions are kicked up to the board of directors. The hope is by that point all emotion, cognitive biases and potential errors have been filtered out of the decision-analysis.

## 2.2 Information Processing Issues

In his book Thinking Fast and Slow, Daniel Kahneman adopts the terms **System 1 and System 2** (originally coined by Keith Stanovich and Richard West) to describe the functioning of the human brain. They do not reside in any particular part of the brain

---

6. Prospect theory, covered later in this chapter, does fit that bill. It was one of the reasons Kahneman was awarded the Nobel Prize in Economics.

but are rather a description of how the brain functions when it makes a decision. System 1 is always active and is responsible for making quick decisions and automatic responses such as routine driving skills, reacting to loud noises, reading facial cues, doing simple mathematics, etc. It is impulsive and intuitive. That is not so say System 1 is primitive, but it acts quickly and spontaneously to stimuli and comes to quick conclusions. We do not have conscious access to System 1. Other characteristics of System 1 include:

- Generating skilled intuitions;

- Making causal connections;

- Suppressing doubt;

- Substituting an easier question for a more difficult one; and

- Over weighting low probabilities.

System 2 on the other hand is the analyzer of complex data and does the heavy lifting when it comes to making weighty decisions. System 2 engages when the decision has the potential for significant risk and reward. It approves the actions of System 1 and can override System 1. System 2 is not good at multi-tasking, requires a lot of energy, and is cautious by nature. System 2 is our aware self.

System 1 is marvelously efficient, but also can jump to quick conclusions. Unfortunately, these quick, intuitive decisions can be wrong. System 1 is where **bias** and information processing issues arise. Bias can be defined as systematic errors occurring in predictable patterns. When making crucial decisions for an organization such as those described later in this book, we strive to get the decision making process into System 2. Organizations take this one step further by having vetting major decisions by senior management, experts in the area of the decision, and even the board of directors. Yet, System 1 does not shut off. We are still subject to its vicissitudes. System 2 may generate a correct answer for us, but we still need to understand the influence System 1 has even when System 2 made the decision. System 1 impacts our decisions through biases, or the interpretation of decisions generated by System 2.

Knowing when someone has engaged their System 2 is critical for discussing the decision with other stakeholders and getting their "buy-in. We all have encountered coworkers or managers who are laser-focused on some problem at hand and don't seem to hear or let alone comprehend what you are saying about another topic. Their System 2 has been engaged and multi-tasking (meaning listening to you) is simply not in the cards. We seem to instinctively know that as well because more often than not we will simply become quiet and wait to finish our conversation until the person completes the first task at hand. *Picking the time to engage other stakeholders in a conversation about a complex decision is critical to gaining acceptance for it.* You must make sure they have engaged their System 2 and it is focused on your decision.

Besides the issues caused by Systems 1 and 2, decision-makers also have limited cognitive capacity. For instance, memory is a critical factor in decision making. We tend to remember unusual items or repeated items. The easier we remember something the easier it can be applied to a decision. We overweight decision factors we remember more easily. To compensate for this shortcoming in today's world, we tend to remember how to access information rather than the information itself. The internet gives us quick access to untold amounts of information. We often don't remember all of the details about a decision attribute, but we remember how to research them.

Aside from dealing with our "split personalities" of Systems 1 and 2 and cognitive limitations decision-makers may suffer from poor information processing caused by other factors. Examples are becoming fatigued or feeling pressured because of deadlines.

The following is not an exhaustive list, but are examples of common processing issues decision-makers should be aware of:

## Overweighting recent evidence

Forecasting is a difficult thing to do under any circumstances, but decision-makers tend to place too much weight on recent evidence and experience. This can make the forecast either too rosy or too pessimistic since there is normally uncertainty in the data being used in the decision making process.[7]

## Overconfidence

Decision-makers tend to be quite optimistic about their own ability to make decisions, to the point where they can exclude other legitimate points of view. Overconfidence can sometimes result from relying on one's intuition too much. One acerbic commentator pointed out how often successful entrepreneurs ignore good business advise by asking, "If you are so smart why aren't you rich?" The point being past success may spur on over-confidence. Needless to say, overconfidence in one's own ability to make decisions can produce bad decisions as critical information can be ignored and doubts are suppressed. Ask Hilary Clinton about her overconfidence in the 2016 American Presidential election.

---

7.  Kahneman and Tversky (1972 and 1973)

Overconfidence of leadership can be disastrous. History is littered with examples of bad decisions made through overconfidence. Custer at the Battle of the Little Big Horn, Hitler invading the Soviet Union, and Varus in Germany are just a few sensationally bad decisions that come to mind. Significantly, each of these military decision-makers had been extremely successful in previous endeavors. In the business world overconfidence can lead corporations to overpay in mergers (Malmendier & Tate, CEO Overconfidence and Corporate Investment, 2004) and a lower, not higher stock price.

Closely related to the over-confidence effect is decision-makers tend to believe desirable outcomes are more probable. Ask anyone who plays the lottery! We overestimate the probability of desirable outcomes, sometimes dismissing the true probability of success.

## Conservatism

Sometimes decision-makers will be too slow or too conservative to change their beliefs. This could cause an under-reaction to a new challenge or environment. The way decision-makers should take into account new information is described by the use of **Bayes Theorem**, a topic for later discussion. Conservatism is a debated subject. Sadly, Kahneman and Tversky proved most people are not very adept Bayesian thinkers and don't handle probability well at all. Rather than failing to extract <u>probabilities</u> from data, decision-makers tend to extract unwarranted <u>certainty</u> from data.

## Emotions

Long thought to be impediments to making clear decisions, recent thinking on the subject suggests emotions are necessary for making a decision.[8] However, moods do impact decisions in interesting ways. Happiness will generally prompt less analysis when making a decision. Sadness will cause more detailed analytical thinking. Overall positive and negative feelings could influence one's perception of the risks and rewards associated with a decision. A feeling of "good" or "bad" may attach to a particular decision. For example, investors may feel "good" about investing in socially responsible corporations or companies interested in social justice even if this isn't the best financial decision for that particular decision-maker.

## Reason-based choice

Decision-makers will often find reasons to make a decision and then justify the decision to themselves and others. In such situations, the decision-maker is vulnerable to making the decision on irrelevant attributes. The decoy effect, described in the next section, is an example of this.

## Decoy effect

Sometimes adding a third option to a set of two options changes the stated preferences for the first two options. A consumer may prefer Product A over Product B. Product C is

---

8. This would not be news to any Star Trek fan. An early episode of the show (dating back to the mid-1960s) had Captain Kirk being split into two versions of himself. One was analytical, the other prone to emotional outbursts. The analytical Kirk could not make a decision.

introduced, with attributes inferior to Product B. This will give some consumers a reason to change their minds and choose Product B. In effect, introducing a new option can give us a new reason to choose the alternative not selected before.

Suppose you are considering the purchase of an office copier. The decision attributes you are using are cost and need for service. The higher cost copier has a relatively low level of service required compared to the more inexpensive model. Both copiers have built-in staplers. You then add a third model into the discussion. It is a similarly inexpensive model but does not include a stapler. The introduction of the third model gives the decision-maker a reason to purchase the second model.[9] Introducing a non-existent decoy into the decision making process is known as the **phantom decoy** effect.

## Compromise effect

Given a range of options, decision-makers will tend to avoid the extreme options. For instance, decision-makers will not choose the highest priced or the lowest quality product.

## Numerical bias effect

Decision-makers will tend to assign a higher value to numerical data than qualitative information. There are tools we can use to deal with numerical data, such as statistics and mathematics. Qualitative information is much more difficult to deal with. This can lead to its underweighting in the decision. In subsequent chapters we will see how we can handle both quantitative and

---

9. As unbelievable as it seems, the decoy effect has been proven again and again in research studies.

qualitative data when making a decision.

## Fallacy of composition

The fallacy of composition assumes what is true of one member of a group will be true of the entire group. Suppose you are at a parade. If you stand on your toes to get a better view of the parade, you generally will. If everyone stands on their toes, then no one gets a better view. Another example of the fallacy of composition is assuming the national budget operates in the same manner a household budget does. Since the government can always print or borrow money, the analogy does not strictly hold.

## Post Hoc Ergo Propter Hoc Fallacy

The human mind loves to make connections, sometimes even if connections should not be made. We observe Event A happening followed by Event B. We see this happen over and over again, and our minds may connect the two events with the process of causation. We begin to assume Event A caused Event B. The sun rises in the morning and birds begin to sing. We assume the rising of the sun gives the birds something to chirp about. While there might be many intervening steps in this process, we have come to expect the rising sun will cause birds to begin singing.

Sometimes the connection between two events can be tenuous at best, unsupported by data. Consider a doctor treating a patient who shows no symptoms after the treatment. The doctor assumes the treatment cured the patient but that might not be the case. Perhaps the patient just became better and would have become better without the treatment. The doctor incorrectly assumed the treatment was the cause of the improvement.

The decision-maker not only has to be careful about assuming direct causation but indirect causation as well. The natural products industry (also known as the botanical or herbal industry) is a big industry not only in the United States but around the world. Medical schools grant degrees in naturopathic medicine where many of these herbal products are used. Unfortunately, natural products have a reputation for somewhat shaky science and extraordinary claims. In the United States, natural and herbal products are regulated as food rather than as drugs because of heavy lobbying. They do not need to go through the same rigorous screening new drugs do. Many outrageous claims about the efficacy of natural products are made simply because there is no way to disprove the claims.

One famous example of indirect causation error was the shark cartilage craze of several decades ago. Doctors and pitchmen were making infomercials claiming there was something special about shark cartilage. Sharks reportedly don't get cancer[10] so many natural products proponents somehow drew the conclusion shark cartilage was the reason. They relied on the cartilage being a **marker** indicating a second event was going to occur, even if the occurrence of the second event could not be explained by the first event. Event A was always accompanied by Event B, even if Event A may not be the cause of Event B.[11] While a marker may have indirect probative value, you need to be careful when using this line of reasoning. Event A was the shark cartilage. Event B was sharks not getting cancer. Ergo, taking shark cartilage pills can help humans avoid cancer! Pharmacies were filling up with bottles of shark cartilage despite the fact some crucial questions were not

---

10. The author cannot confirm or deny this assertion. He is simply reporting it as it was reported in the day.

11. Statistically, two events can be correlated but neither might cause the other.

answered, such as "How does this work?" or, "If it does work, how do I know each capsule is an efficacious dosage?"

In short, claims of causation need to be critically examined by decision-makers.[12] Even today, there are natural products being sold purportedly improving our sex lives, making us lose weight, providing anti-viral protection and improving our mood. One has to wonder if these botanical products did work as advertised, why isn't everyone taking them?[13]

## The Framing Effect

We saw how the framing effect works in the first chapter. The decision-maker evaluates some information or attribute as being important while evaluating other information as less important, even if the valued and devalued information are equivalent. For example, a person accused of a crime might react very differently to how a plea bargain is being posed. The accused may very well consider a plea bargain if the question is framed as a 20% chance of conviction rather than an 80% chance of acquittal.

Another type of framing centers on the **status quo** of a situation. With everything else being equal, the decision-maker has a tendency to pick the status quo. It is often regarded as kind of a "sure thing". Consider how infrequently people change their life insurance policies. It is done so infrequently the agent who writes the policy is paid a very high percentage of the first-year

---

12. Time and space do not permit me to go into detail here, but there are wonderful philosophical treatises on this subject.

13. Many years ago, I overheard a natural products executive say every company in the industry was looking for three things: a cure for male baldness, a sure-fire method of enhancing sexual potency and something that would melt the pounds away without needing to go on a diet. Needless to say, the entire industry is still looking for these three wonder drugs.

commission. The insurance company can count on the policy premiums for years to come.

The status quo framing effect is closely related to the **anchoring** effect. The status quo becomes an anchor and adjustments are made from that particular initial position. Anchoring impacts negotiations, as the status quo becomes the anchor for further adjustments.

## The Overchoice effect

This occurs when the decision-maker is presented with too many options, many of which are acceptable. The degree of effort or even the contemplated amount of effort required can often cause the decision-maker to simply "shut-down" or "punt" on the decision. Classical economic theory suggests the more choices offered to the decision-maker, the better. However, the effect so many and varied choices may have on the decision-maker is cognitive overload.

An example of this principle is employee benefit plans. You may notice health insurance and employee savings plans have a limited number of options to choose from. In many cases having a larger number of options causes the decision-maker (in this case, the employee) to simply not participate. It is too much work for the employee, who just gives up. A large number of choices can create anxiety and the fear of making the wrong choice. Without sufficient employee participation, a benefit plan may run afoul of labor or tax regulations and cause a great deal of distress for the sponsoring company. By reducing the number of options, employee participation generally goes up as the decision become manageable for the employee.

There are situations where the decision-maker wants to have a significant amount of options. The first is where computing power or artificial intelligence is available to assist the decision-maker. The second is where the decision-maker has an articulated ideal, an idea of the perfect solution to the problem. A large variety of options can be handled by the decision-maker at that point through a "sort and filter" process. Any option not reasonably close to the ideal solution is quickly jettisoned. This comparison process is much easier for the decision-maker than a detail review of attributes.

## Fear of missing out

"Fear of missing out", or **FOMO** for short is an apprehension of not being included in some event. For instance, an investor may choose to buy a particular stock because it is popular, and he fears missing the gain from a potentially great investment. FOMO can also lead to adhering to the **conventional wisdom** when making a decision. It is hard to criticize a decision-maker if everyone else is making the same mistake.

## Regret avoidance

Individuals will tend to regret decisions turning out badly more if the decision does not follow the aforementioned conventional wisdom. This could be attributed to either self-censure for not "making the obvious choice" or the external criticism a decision-maker may feel if an unconventional decision turns out to be incorrect. The sports world abounds with such managerial miscues, as does the business world. Head coaches and business executives can be regularly seen in the media explaining these decisions, why the decisions did not work out, and their regret at making such a poor decision.

## Affect

Certain decisions just make us feel good and certain decisions do not. Our judgments can be influenced by feelings of liking something or not. For instance, we might purchase one type of car because we have strong feelings of like for the particular brand or what it represents. Perhaps you purchase the new version of a car you have had pleasant experiences with, or you bought with your first paycheck after you graduated from college. In both cases the car brings back positive memories and "good' feelings.

Imagine you are the parent of several children and decide to purchase a Corvette. This may not be a particularly practical decision, especially since you really need a second family car, but the decision makes you feel good, so you are naturally attracted to it. The alternative is purchasing an minivan. This has certain connotations such as "soccer mom" attached to it, and it is certainly not your self-image. You dislike those connotations, so you decide on the very sporty car model instead, even though you know it's impractical and will not accommodate the demands family life.

# 2.3 Prospect Theory

Prospect theory was the revolutionary economic theory proposed by **Daniel Kahneman** and Amos Tversky. This theory, along with his other work in behavioral economics[14] earned Kahneman the Noble Prize in Economics in 2002. Sadly, Tversky has passed away prior to the date of the award, and the Nobel Prize is not awarded posthumously. In many ways, prospect theory turned the economic world on its head and propelled the authors into the forefront of decision science. The appeal of prospect theory was it could be demonstrated, and it generated predictions, answering one of the major criticisms of behavioral economics and finance.

**Daniel Bernoulli** (1700-1782), a Swiss mathematician and pioneer in the fields of statistics and utility, noticed the more we have of something the less sensitive we are to changes in it. An astute reader will already notice this insight is directly connected to the concept of **marginal utility**, or the incremental satisfaction we gain from having an additional unit of some good producing utility (satisfaction) in us. This relationship can be graphed. As we move up and down a marginal utility curve our satisfaction changes in a non-linear manner. The following graph illustrates this proposition. As the input of good X increases, our utility, or satisfaction, increases at a diminishing rate.

---

14. Behavioral economics is a branch of behavioralist studies, a systematic attempt to understand human behavior.

**Figure 2.1**

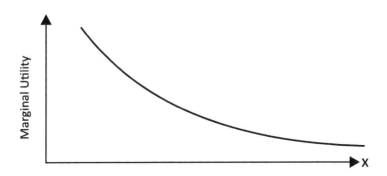

Kahneman and Tversky's insight was gain and loss (movement along the curve) are not perceived in the same way. A loss produced more pain (or is perceived much more sharply) than an equivalent amount of gain. In fact, they discovered a loss was felt approximately twice as much as an equivalent amount of gain.

**Figure 2.2**

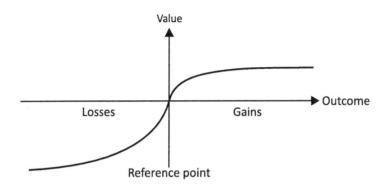

In the above diagram, the slope of the total utility curve to the left of the origin is much steeper than the slope of the total utility curve to the right of the origin. This indicates the decision-maker experiences more pain from the loss of one unit near the origin than the amount of utility generated by possessing one more unit of the same good. This lead Kahneman and Tversky to the insight decision-makers tend to be **risk averse**. Gaining one more unit at the risk of losing one unit would not be an acceptable risk to most people.

Prospect theory has three main tenants:

1. The curve demonstrated above has a reference point of zero, but the "origin" could be any particular starting number. For example, the "origin" could be our life savings. The utility and disutility from gains and losses would operate in the same way using the total amount of savings as the reference point. We always evaluate a decision relative to "something else" and that "something else" is always relative and contextual. In this example, it is the total amount of life savings. Sadly, we may even use bad reference points to make decisions, something a decision-maker needs to be on guard against. This sentiment is captured by the common aphorism "the bar is low" when someone is making a decision in a bad situation.

2. The theory of marginal utility applies to changes from the origin point.

3. However, the slope of the curve is steeper to the left of the origin point. Decision-makers feel loss more sharply than they do gain. Hence, we can draw the conclusion people are indeed risk adverse.

This "steep" feeling of loss has been named the **endowment effect**. We place psychological values on our possessions. Once we have something, we simply do not want to give it up and experience the pain of the sharp descent along the prospect theory utility curve. Have you ever attempted to negotiate the purchase of a piece of property from someone and they attach a price to it entirely above its market value? This is an example of the endowment effect at work.

Prospect theory has many applications. Companies will try to keep up a steady barrage of good news in the form of press releases. Each new press release moves investors along the steepest part of the total utility curve to the right of the starting point. Conversely, companies also try to aggregate bad news and announce it at one time, the so-called **Big Bath**. Releasing negative information slowly and over time continually moves investors over the steepest part of the marginal utility curve to the left of the starting point.[15] They feel the sharp pain of the bad news as the stock price begins to drift south over and over again. Corporate CEOs continually allowing bad news to dribble out from the company often face very short tenures.

## 2.4 Mental Accounting

**Richard Thaler (b. 1948)**, winner of the Nobel prize in Economics in 2017 for his work in behavioral economics, coined the term **mental accounting** to describe how people categorize the uses of their money and resources. An example of this is how

---

15. Not to mention the fact delaying the release of material bad news into the market could also be a violation of SEC rules.

we divide our monthly income into different buckets. We do the mental accounting and budget so much for our rent, food, entertainment, transportation, etc. A completely rational person would understand each dollar of income is equivalent to any other dollar of income. In point of fact, we do not operate that way. We try to stay within our mental accounting boundaries even if there is no apparent reason to do so other than we have set those boundaries for ourselves.

To illustrate this process, two people are going to the theater.[16] The price of admission is $20. One person purchases the ticket in advance and loses it on the way to the theater. A second person loses a $20 bill on the way to the theater before he has purchased his ticket. Which is more likely to purchase a second ticket? Both individuals are in exactly the same position. They have both lost an equivalent amount of money. However, the person who lost the ticket is less likely to purchase a new theater ticket. They have already expended the money allotted for entertainment by their mental accounting and tend not to buy a new ticket.

Another example of how mental accounting affects decisions is the partitioning of the total cost of any item for sale could change people's preferences for that item. This is why many merchants do not include an "all-in" price for a product and divide the price into the cost of the product, the shipping cost, and the sales tax. Consumers generally view the second option more favorably even if the final total price is the same to the consumer, who should be ambivalent between the two under classical economic theory.

The way employees look at their paychecks demonstrates how mental accounting works. 401(k) plans are very popular. The employer withholds funds from the employee and deposits it

_____

16. This example is also from Thinking Fast and Slow

directly into a savings plan. The employee learns to live without the savings and begins to build a nest egg. An even stronger example is the over withholding of income taxes so a refund will be obtained when the final tax return is filed for the year. Many taxpayers look at this as a form of forced savings and have also learned to live with a lower net paycheck. Most accountants will tell you this is a not a particularly good way to save, but it does have the virtue of being easy to do. When you apply prospect theory, you can see why people over withhold. They simply do not want to feel the pain of making a payment at the end of the year if they owe taxes.

The **theory of double-entry mental accounting** links the dual effects of the pleasure of consuming with the painful effects of payment. Paying cash couples a painful experience (losing money) with the pleasure of purchasing something we want and makes that purchase less likely. This accounts for the popularity of installment payment plans and credit cards. The pain of purchasing is decoupled from the pain of consuming.

# Chapter Summary

◆ The economic man makes decisions based on perfect information, adequate time to process data and alternatives and in a perfectly rational way.

◆ These assumptions have been challenged by the behavioral branches of economics, finance, and psychology. The theory of System 1 and System 2 processing is one such example.

◆ There is a long list of cognitive biases and processing issues decision-makers face. They must be on guard to filter these out of the decision making process.

◆ An organization must have controls in place to help filter out biases and processing errors by decision-makers.

◆ Prospect theory states decision-makers start with a reference point. A loss from that reference point is felt far more sharply than an equivalent amount of gain from the same reference point.

◆ Mental accounting claims our decisions are influenced by how we allocate our resources. Our minds "budget" resources and we make decisions based on that budgeting.

◆ Despite all of these criticisms of the economic man, this model of decision making is still the predominant operational theory of economists.

# Discussion Questions

1. Some of the characteristics of Systems 1 and 2 were discussed in this chapter. What are some of the other characteristics of this system?

2. What are some of the organizational structures your organization has in place to prevent someone's System 1 processing from "hijacking" a major decision?

3. Can you think of a decision you made recently influenced by affect? If it was a monetary decision, was it impacted by your "discretionary income"?

4. How influenced are you by prospect theory? Without any additional facts, would you agree to the flip of a coin where you received $150 for heads and lost $100 if it was tails? Suppose you only had $100. Would you accept this bet?

5. How susceptible are you to the endowment effect? If there was volatility in the stock market, would you "ride" out a downturn in the hopes of future recovery or profit, or would you leave the market at the first chance if you knew volatility lay ahead?

---

*Solutions to the above questions can be downloaded from*
*the* **Online Resources** *section of this book on*
**www.vibrantpublishers.com**

---

*This page is intentionally left blank*

# Chapter 3

# Gathering Data: How Much is Enough?

Good decision analysis and decision making relies on data. How much data is enough? The theoretical and practical considerations of data gathering for decision making are discussed in this chapter.

## 3.1 Speed of a Decision

The decision making process does not exist in a vacuum. Time is one element. All things being considered, the quicker a decision is made the better. The speed with which a decision is made can affect its acceptance and implementation. However, the decision-maker must take into account all relevant information and shouldn't make a decision before such data is available, despite the fact System 1 will often come to an intuitive decision. All of this begs the question, when does a decision-maker know if all relevant data has been obtained?

American courts will not hear a case until it is "ripe", meaning all of the facts should be evident and mature before a decision can be reached. This same principal applies to the decision making process. No decision should be made without sufficient information. Nevertheless, the modern world will not afford decision-makers the luxury of time in many situations. Decisions often need to be made quickly and under conditions of uncertainty. How does one know when enough information has been accumulated to support a decision?

Economic theory affords an answer to this problem through marginal cost and marginal benefit analysis.[17] Recall economic theory holds decisions should be made "**at the margin**." The marginal benefit of additional information is the improvement in the decision based on obtaining this information. The marginal cost of obtaining the additional information includes not only the incremental **out of pocket costs** but the **opportunity costs** as well. The marginal benefit of obtaining the incremental information should never exceed the marginal cost of the incremental data.

Marginal costs tend not to rise in a straight-line. They increase at an ever-expanding rate while marginal benefit (in this case the additional benefit from the additional information) decreases sharply over the relevant range.

---

17. The mathematically minded will understand the term marginal is shorthand for the derivative. The derivative of the cost function (cost curve) is the marginal cost and the derivative of the revenue (utility) function is the marginal revenue or the marginal utility.

**Figure 3.1**

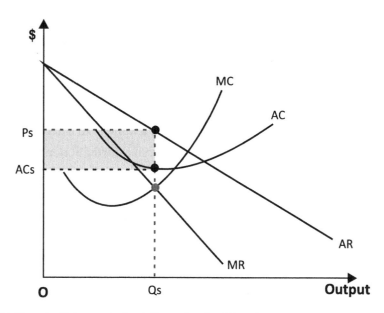

This Photo by Unknown Author is licensed under CC BY-SA

As the graph demonstrates, the cost of obtaining additional information rises at an increasing rate while the marginal benefit of the additional information to the decision decreases.

In classical economics, the decision-maker possesses perfect information about any economic decision before it is made. As we have seen that may not always be the case due to the cognitive limitations of the decision-maker. We can now add an additional limiting factor to our discussion of decision analysis and decision making. The cost (including the time spent as an opportunity cost) of obtaining perfect information rises precipitously and becomes prohibitive.

As a practical matter, when does a decision-maker know when to cease gathering information? Here are some practical guidelines:

1. **Some decisions can be deferred until a required point in time**. Remember the judicial ripeness doctrine the chapter opened with. Some facts become available over time. While a speedy decision is generally preferred to a delayed one, certain critical information may be available to a decision-maker only through time. Additional information may become available only as time progresses. Waiting until the last minute before making a decision ensures all available information is factored into the decision and is a viable strategy. Additionally, quick intuitive decisions often tend to be incorrect.

2. **Conduct a cost-benefit analysis of obtaining additional information**. This determination can often be made by critical thinking and questioning. What is the incremental benefit of gathering additional information? Under what circumstances can additional information render my decision incorrect and what is the probability of that happening? When adopting a purposeful strategy of waiting for additional information, the decision-maker must always understand the costs delaying may cause the organization. The potential damages must be included in the cost-benefit analysis.

3. **Understand the decision rule**. The decision rule itself may dictate the amount of information you need for the decision. For instance, a criminal trial requiring a "**beyond the reasonable doubt**" standard of evidence will often require much more information than a civil lawsuit where a preponderance of evidence standard applies. A

pharmaceutical company requesting permission to market a new drug will need to prove the efficaciousness of the drug by using a statistical method, requiring a given sample size. Approaching the government regulators before obtaining this type of data and performing the required analysis would be pure folly.

# Chapter Summary

◆ In the modern business world, the faster a decision is made the better-off the organization usually is.

◆ Despite this general rule, the decision-maker must make sure she has sufficient information to make a valid decision.

◆ While classical economic theory states decisions are made with perfect information, this is not always true. The marginal cost of obtaining information rises quickly, often exceeding the marginal benefit of obtaining such data. Sometimes the cost of obtaining incremental data becomes prohibitive.

◆ Data relevant to the decision may become available over time. Knowing when the costs of waiting begin should be factored into the cost-benefit analysis.

# Discussion Questions

1. Are you a patient decision-maker?

2. Do you wait to obtain necessary data before making a critical decision?

> *Solutions to the above questions can be downloaded from*
> *the* **Online Resources** *section of this book on*
> **www.vibrantpublishers.com**

*This page is intentionally left blank*

# Chapter **4**

# Group Mechanics

> Decision-makers don't operate in a vacuum. Groups
> may be used to gather information and assist in
> the decision making process. In this chapter, we will learn
> about some of the common techniques used to facilitate
> group decision making as well as some of the dangers of
> groupthink.

## 4.1 Introduction

Complex decisions are seldom made by one decision-maker.
We have seen individual decision-makers have cognitive
limitations and biases. Organizations should have checks and
balances in the decision making process, ensuring decisions have
been vetted and are mistake and bias-free. This chapter takes up
the question of how and why it is sometimes necessary to include
a group in the decision process.

A major reason groups are used in decision-processes is to
generate ideas that become either data or decision options. The
second reason is while all stakeholders in a decision may want the

best for the organization as a whole, they may have competing individual or departmental goals or different opinions. For instance, the corporate counsel may have a much different view of a risky product development than the sales department. Using a decision making group can help bring everyone's concerns to the table for discussion and resolution.

## 4.2 Informal Consultations

The simplest method of gathering information from other stakeholders is through informal consultations. In such situations, the decision-maker usually but not always reserves the final decision but will attempt to gather as much information as possible through informal discussions with other stakeholders. Other parties the decision-maker may want to consult are owners, bankers, creditors, attorneys, accountants, unions, etc. Informal consultation could include discussion with thought leaders, or those having expert knowledge and prestige in their particular field and are often independent of the organization. Thought leaders typically come from management consulting firms, colleges, trade associations, etc.

Different stakeholders will have different degrees of interest in the decision and will often hold various power levers. They may also have different levels of authority within the organization. Identifying and consulting with these groups, even informally, can be the difference between success or failure of the decision. Different types of authority are:

- **Formal power**–This resides with individuals who could as a matter of corporate organization or law block, change, or help implement a decision

- **Informal power**–This type of power could originate in personal charisma, seniority, social status or any number of other factors. A person with informal power could have a position anywhere in the organization. Finding and consulting these leaders can be important for persuading others to agree with and help implement any decision.

- **Knowledge power**–A person may not have formal authority within an organization but may have expertise in the particular matter being discussed. These are often people who have seniority in the organization and have worked in and on the areas being impacted by the decision.

## 4.3 Formal Consultations

Many organizations wisely provide a structured review process for any major decision. Decision-makers often consult with the senior executives of the company and possibly the board of directors about any strategic decisions. An interesting type of formal consultation occurs when the power to make the decision is vested in one or a handful of people. In such a case, there may not be an effective legal barrier to making a bad decision. One way to apply a "brake" to bad decisions in this situation is through an institutionalized advisor or an advisory board. While the decision-maker retains the final authority to make a decision, the advisory board can provide critical data and ideas. In some cases, consultation with an advisory body is necessary before the decision is finalized. An example of this is the Roman Catholic Church, where diocesan bishops wield almost total power over the local church. Certain major decisions though require consultation with his advisors before the decision is announced. The advisors act as a type of "speed-bump" in the decision process by providing information and perhaps other proposed solutions. Ultimately though, the decision is the bishop's.[18]

# 4.4 Brainstorming

Brainstorming is a method of generating ideas to solve a problem. It involves a group of people quickly suggesting a number of options for a decision. The rules for a brainstorming session should be:

- There are no bad ideas;

- Ideas should be made without regard to rank or hierarchy;

- The goal should be to generate as many ideas as possible;

- Wait to evaluate ideas until the end of the session.

Brainstorming has many applications in decision making and is being used as a new approach in fraud detection. Independent auditors were previously required to hold a planning meeting prior to the beginning of the audit. They are now required to brainstorm during the meeting about potential sources of fraud and its concealment in an organization.

There are three types of brainstorming:

- **Open brainstorming**–are unstructured sessions with few rules.

---

18. Those familiar with Catholic canon law will recognize these groups as the Finance Council, the Consultors, and the Presbyteral Council.

- **Round Robin brainstorming**–Participants are assigned homework ahead of time. Each participant presents their own ideas and each participant gets a turn.

- **Electronic brainstorming**–Suggestions are depersonalized as the originator of the idea remains anonymous.[19]

The brainstorming session should not stop to evaluate each idea as they are being proposed. Stopping or slowing down the flow of the meeting will reduce the number of ideas. Evaluation of the ideas should begin at the end of the brainstorming session.

Common problems encountered in brainstorming are:

- **One person can dominate the discussion**. Usually this is someone who possesses some type of status or authority in the group.

- **The tug of war problem.** In a tug of war consisting of two people both will work as hard as they can to win the game. Adding an additional person to each side does not double the total effort of the team. One or both players will reduce their efforts. The reduction in effort will become more pronounced as additional people are added to the teams. The same can occur as more and more people are added to the brainstorming session. Less effort from disengagement could occur because of the larger team.

- **Groupthink** can be become a problem. We turn to this issue next.

---

19. Ramos, M. "Auditors' Responsibility for Fraud Detection" Journal of Accountancy (January 2003).

# 4.5 Groupthink

Anyone who has worked in a large organization has experienced groupthink. This disfunction causes little consideration being given to ideas contradicting the group consensus. Often, they are rejected outright. In extreme cases, options may not even be brought forward because of group pressure. For instance, faculty meetings at any large college are often dominated by deans and senior tenured professors with any decision adopted appearing to have near unanimous consent.

What types of groups tend to fall into groupthink?

1. Very cohesive groups and those insulated from outside influences.

2. People who have been working together for a period of time.

3. A lack of process in searching for options and their evaluation.

4. Domination by one or a few members, generally with some type of authority. The rest of the participants often fall into line behind the leader.

5. Lack of diversity in membership, whether it be gender, race, or any other affiliation.

6. Situations causing pressure to conform and avoid conflict lead to groupthink.

What are some of the outcomes of groupthink?

1. Rationalization of a chosen course of action;

2. Pressure on those in the minority to adhere to the final decision whether it is right or wrong;

3. Excessive optimism or pessimism about its outcome;

4. An illusion of having a unanimous consensus; and

5. Greater potential for an incorrect decision.

Many of the problems religious organizations encounter can be attributed to groupthink. They are frequently dominated by a leadership group entirely homogeneous in its composition, working together for a long period of time and dominated by one or a few leaders with formal authority. Coupled with an often-weak control environment, the religious organization may not regulate itself appropriately or not respond to changing circumstances. Similarly, the lack of diversity in the corporate world has resulted in a major push for electing woman and other previously disenfranchised people to boards of director in major corporations. This is not only appropriate from a social justice perspective but also because varied experiences and knowledge brings about better decisions.

Groupthink can cause a certain blindness to new and important information and a failure to assess the available options completely. Sometimes groupthink causes risks to be underestimated or minimized, underscoring the importance of having contingency plans if the decision turns out poorly.

The psychologist Gary Klein proposed a remedy to the groupthink problem called the **premortem**. Before the decision is finalized, the group is reassembled and told to imagine the decision turned out poorly. The members are instructed to write a short narrative about what went wrong and how the decision could turn out so poorly. In this way the group is forced to confront its own fears about the decision and deal with any obstacles it can reasonably foresee before the decision is finalized and its implementation.

# Chapter Summary

◆ There are various ways to gather information and ideas from a group when making a decision. Consultation is one way to proceed. It can be done via an informal or a formal process.

◆ Brainstorming is one method to generate ideas and options. Group members propose as many ideas as possible. Evaluation of the ideas should occur at the end of the session.

◆ Any decision making body needs to be concerned about groupthink. A diverse group of decision-makers is the best protection against groupthink. Consider using the premortem to reduce groupthink.

# Discussion Questions

1. Describe a groupthink situation you were involved in. How did the decision turn out? What were the causes of the groupthink? How could it have been avoided?

2. Have you ever participated in a brainstorming session? What was the topic? Did the session generate enough ideas? Did the suggestions flow smoothly or were they evaluated as they were made? Did hierarchy and rank interfere with the discussions?

> *Solutions to the above questions can be downloaded from*
> *the* **Online Resources** *section of this book on*
> **www.vibrantpublishers.com**

# Chapter 5

# Scenario Planning and Prediction Markets

Is there a difference between risk and uncertainty? If so, how does a decision-maker deal with each of them? In this chapter, we will review some of the common techniques decision-makers use to deal with uncertainty.

The economist **Frank Knight (1885-1972)**[20] drew a distinction between **risk** and **uncertainty**. According to Knight, risk could be quantified. Uncertainty cannot. Uncertainty comes in many forms, including a technological breakthrough, a sudden shift in law or regulatory focus, or even a natural phenomenon such as the COVID-19 pandemic. Uncertainty will be discussed in this chapter. Risk will be dealt with later the book.

---

20. Frank Knight was a member of the influential "Chicago" school of economics.

# 5.1 Scenario Planning

**Scenario planning** recognizes unique events are extremely difficult to forecast but can and do occur. These types of events, usually extremely disruptive to the organization have been labeled **black swans** by Nassim Nicholas Taleb, author of the Black Swan: The Impact of the Highly Improbable. Black swans were thought to be impossible until one was spotted. In the business world we often think certain events are not possible or have a very small probability of happening. Occasionally, they do in fact happen. As a result, even the best guesses about the future can turn out to be very, very wrong no matter how hard decision-makers try. Scenarios are not a forecast of the future. They are an examination of possibilities encompassing a wide range of possible futures. Each of the scenarios has a low probability of occurring but the scope and the range of the scenarios considered is an attempt to plan for future uncertainties. Through the scenario planning process, the organization tries to convert uncertainty into risk.

Scenario planning begins with current information for the base year and then proceeds to a predetermined horizon year. For example, an organization may do scenario planning in conjunction with its multi-year strategic plan. As each year lapses, the scenarios will be updated for the for a succeeding year. For instance, in a five-year planning horizon, the lapse of one year will bring about the update of scenario planning for the fifth succeeding year. Next, the decision-maker defines the critical uncertainties the organization may face based on known trends and the changes in these trends. Unique events will be considered at this stage as well. Examples of some trends all scenario planners need to take into account are demographic shifts in its customer and labor markets, projected technological improvements such as the growth in computing power, political changes including changes in regulation and taxation, evolving cultural values, and economic fluctuations. This is not an all-inclusive list and should be tailored to the individual circumstances of each organization.

Besides using scenario planning for strategic planning, there are other times when it should be considered, such as when an organization believes there is a significant amount of uncertainty is in its future. Perhaps there have been many unsettling surprises in the its past or in the entire industry. Consider the airline industry. In the last twenty years alone, it has been forced to ground its aircraft by terrorist activity and a pandemic. Airlines are particularly sensitive to oil prices. These prices have surged and declined precipitously over the last several decades, including a very brief time when the price of a barrel of oil was negative. Virtual conferencing has reduced the need for business travel. In short, the airline industry has been buffeted by a series of one-off events and other trends when considered together indicate a dangerous amount of uncertainty in its future. Such a confluence of events should push scenario planning to the top of the strategic planning methodologies.

Another situation scenario planning could be of great interest to an organization is where strong differences of opinion about the future of the organization exist in its management or board of directors. Scenario planning can assist management in analyzing the consequences of each proposed course of action, creating some consensus among management. It is especially important if the intent of the scenario planning is to reconcile disparate opinions and insure any minority opinions are heard, analyzed and considered.

If done correctly there are several helpful outcomes from scenario planning. The organization might uncover opportunities it can exploit or develop an appreciation for threats developing on the planning horizon. After completing scenario planning, management can move forward with its decision, confident it has considered at least the foreseeable uncertainties it may face.

## 5.2 Prediction Markets

Another but somewhat controversial method of attempting to deal with uncertainty is through the use of **prediction markets**. In many places, prediction markets are illegal and considered contrary to public purpose. They have also acquired a somewhat odious reputation since the United States Department of Defense floated a trial balloon in 2003 (shortly after the 9/11 incidents) to use prediction markets in anticipating future terror attacks. This was swiftly abandoned after fierce public reaction.

Prediction markets use market forces to predict the resolution of uncertainties. They operate by collecting the consensus of a large group of participants, who in effect buy and sell options contracts on future events. There has been research suggesting prediction markets have been successful. James Surowiecki, the author of The Wisdom of the Crowd points out the entire process relies on diversity of information and independence of the participants to produce their results.

The most famous currently operating prediction market is the University of Iowa Electronic market, operating under an exemption from the United States federal government. It has been used since the 1988 to predict the results of the American presidential election with good results but was spectacularly incorrect about the 2016 election. Even when wrong though, prediction markets can provide valuable insight about what the populace is thinking. The increase in computing power and the use of Big Data will make prediction markets a more common decision analysis tool in the future.

The stock market can be considered one form of prediction market and it has been defined as a leading economic indicator. The efficient market hypothesis claims stock prices accurately reflect the information about companies in the market.[21] A recent and for many people  painful example of how well this prediction market works was the precipitous fall in the stock market before the full impact of the COVID-19 pandemic was  acknowledged by the United States government. The stock market plunged well before the pandemic killed and affected hundreds of thousands of Americans. It had anticipated a horrible uncertainty and factored this into stock prices.

---

21. There are several forms of the EMH, with the strong form of the hypothesis stating all information about a stock, including insider information, has already been factored into its price.

## Chapter Summary

◆ Risk and uncertainty are terms often used interchangeably. The distinction is risk can be measured through the use of probability and uncertainty can't.

◆ Black Swan events create uncertainty because they are complete surprises and have a major impact on organizations.

◆ One way an organization can deal with uncertainty is through scenario planning. The probability of any one particular scenario playing out may be small, but cumulatively there is a possibility at least one scenario will occur.

◆ Scenario planning tries to convert uncertainty into risk.

◆ Another but more controversial method for dealing with uncertainty is by using prediction markets. This will become more common in the future.

# Discussion Questions

1. One common form of scenario planning many organizations do is disaster recovery planning. Does your organization have a disaster recovery plan? If so, what are the elements of that plan and what does it encompass? How often is it updated?

2. You are an airline executive taking part in a scenario planning exercise. Describe some of the scenarios you want to consider.

---

*Solutions to the above questions can be downloaded from the* **Online Resources** *section of this book on* **www.vibrantpublishers.com**

*This page is intentionally left blank*

# Chapter **6**

# Heuristics and Programmed Decisions

Is extensive decision analysis necessary for each decision? How should we make the many smaller decisions we face? This chapter deals with some of the "fast and frugal" methods we use to make decisions in our everyday lives.

## 6.1 Heuristics

You are planning your first vacation in a long time. Where do you plan to go? (Hopefully, not on the cruise ship discussed in Chapter 1!) Your lifelong ambition is to visit every major league baseball stadium in the United States. What are some of the factors you consider when choosing which baseball city to visit this year? That list could include decision attributes such as:

1. Whether you have been there before;

2. The amount of time you have available to make the trip;

3. What teams are playing in the various stadiums;

4. The cost of the trip;

5. The time of year; and

6. Are you going alone or with a friend?

Each person will have a different set of criteria for making this decision. What about a typical business decision?

Suppose the office copier lease is about to expire. You can either renew the current lease for the same equipment or select a new copier. What are some of the considerations you take into account when making this decision? They could include:

1. Do you need to make two sided copies?

2. Do you need multiple paper trays?

3. Do you need to make color copies?

4. Do not need the copier to "sort and staple"?

5. What is the cost?

6. How reliable is the copier?

7. Will there be adequate service if the copier breaks down?

8. How fast does service arrive if the copier malfunctions?

These two decisions are complex because they have many attributes, but they also have one thing in common: they don't entail a lot of reward or risk. If your goal is to go to every baseball stadium in the United States, there is very little risk of picking the "wrong" stadium in any one particular year. You will eventually end up at that stadium anyway, if not this year then sometime in the future. Choosing the "wrong" office copier will not ordinarily bring an organization to its knees but could often cause some mild inconvenience.

Organizations face these types of decisions having limited reward and risk every day. Making an occasional mistake is acceptable. Typical examples of such decisions include seemingly mundane choices regarding what color the office should be painted or what color should the carpets be. While decisions like these seem trivial, they still need to be made. Decision-makers have a limited amount of time to spend on decisions such as these, so they need fast and efficient methods of making choices.[22]

**Heuristics** are quick decision tools ideal for such decisions. They are the result of the decision-maker's bounded rationality since the decision-maker has limited cognitive ability. There is only so much time and energy that can be exerted on any one decision since there are many other decisions to be made. Heuristics often result in approximate or satisfactory decisions, rather than the "optimal" decision if that even exists in the given situation.[23] Using heuristics is often made all the more compelling since they are grounded in the decision-makers' knowledge of the particular circumstances and environment they are operating in. Heuristics often result in "rules of thumb" used to provide quick answers for problems.

---

22. Sadly, decisions such as who is allocated what office space or how reserved parking spots are distributed can take on a life of their own. Some organizations spend an inordinate amount of time on such decisions to the detriment of more important things like strategic planning. Organizations often deal with such conundrums by programmed decision making, a topic taken up in another chapter. For instance, the type of office and its furnishings an executive is given depends on the rank of the individual. The decision is made once and for all and does not have to be revisited each time it needs to be made.

23. The color of the office walls or the carpet would seem to fall into this category.

Let's look at a very common example of a heuristic decision methodology. Everyone at one point in their lives has made a pros and cons list. In the unlikely possibility you have not, a **pros and cons** list is simply that: on one side of the paper you list all of the advantages of a proposed course of action, and on the other side you list all of its disadvantages. This is certainly one way to approach a decision, but it also has clearly recognized deficiencies, including each pro and con could be treated with equal weight. In other words, some of the listed advantages may be far more important than other advantages but this method does not explicitly recognize that. Also, how do you make a decision if the net pros and cons are "very close"?

As "rules of thumb", heuristics should not be used for larger or riskier decisions where more formal analysis is needed. No one should make a major corporate decision based simply on a pros and cons list or a rule of thumb. Heuristics are more often applied when there is one decision-maker. In such situations the decision often does not have to be justified to higher management or a board of directors. Management may ask subordinates to handle a particular problem or issue and either specify the heuristic to be used or ask how the decision was arrived at after it is made. Either way, the use of an acceptable heuristic saves senior management time.

Heuristics can be divided into **compensatory** or **non-compensatory heuristics**. A compensatory strategy allows the decision-maker to compensate for poor performance on one attribute with superior performance on another.

For instance, when judging the skill of a baseball player scouts traditionally looked at "five tools".[24] A deficiency in one skill could be compensated for by superior performance in another. Non-compensatory strategies to not allow that. Each attribute must achieve at least a minimum level of acceptability or the entire option will be rejected. Using a compensatory strategy will often require a higher level of cognitive activity and energy than non-compensatory strategies.

The first question that may come to a decision-maker's mind is **what did we do last time?** This heuristic works well when the previous selection worked satisfactorily and there are no major criticisms of the previous decision. It also works well when a study or investigation had been done to make the previous selection. The decision-maker will assess the need to repeat the study. If there are no changes in the decision attributes there may be no need to repeat the extended study. The decision-maker will select the option based on the study.

The "what did we do last time" heuristic does save time and effort since a new analysis is not required. However, the decision-maker does need to make sure the decision attributes have not changed. For instance, technological advances in the copier industry, new products and new vendors may not be adequately considered when using this heuristic.

The decision-maker will also remember certain good or bad experiences with copiers the company has previously leased. These experiences will guide the decision-maker in her choice of

---

24. For those true baseball fans, they are speed, arm strength, fielding, hitting for average, and hitting for power. Players concentrate on improving all five skills to increase the odds of reaching the major leagues. Some skills are more highly valued than others. Methods of balancing these attributes are demonstrated in later chapters.

product. The decision-maker may remember a "good" experience with Copier A, but a "poor" experience with Copier B. A new Copier A will be selected. The major deficiency of the **availability heuristic** is its reliance on subjective experience. Our judgments are influenced by how easy it is to recall certain events. We tend to remember extraordinary events and not mundane details. Alternatives may be rejected if the decision-maker doesn't remember certain positive events or recalls negative facts about the copier. The events recalled may not be associated with any meaningful decision attribute of the product. Easily recalled events are also not necessarily the most probable event. More easily remembered events are judged to be more probable. This could produce a false correlation. For instance, the breakdown of the otherwise reliable Copier B during a critical project may cause enough unpleasant memories to disqualify the selection of Copier B in the future. We begin to make up stories about Copier B in our minds about it not being particularly reliable, even if statistically it was. The stories we make up by connecting various easily recalled events can often replace judgements of probability. They become our reality and become an attribute of the decision.

The **recognition heuristic** is another common decision process. The decision-maker will choose a recognized option before one that is not recognized. Copier A is manufactured by Company X, which has a sterling reputation for reliability and service. Copier B was produced by a relative newcomer to the industry. Since the decision-maker recognized Company X and its reputation, copier A will be selected. The reputation of Company X may be unwarranted, but it still influenced the decision-maker. The recognized option was chosen instead of a newcomer.

The recognition heuristic is often used to select technology where the decision-maker has very little experience or expertise.

The decision -maker will often have no reference point to make such an evaluation. The reputation of the vendor and the fact their products are being used in many places is a signal to the decision-maker this is an acceptable choice. If the decision does not work out well, the decision- maker can always defend it on the widespread use of the copier by other companies. It was a "safe" decision when it was made.

What happens if neither option is recognized? Usually, the decision-maker will then focus on one of the attributes of the decision and choose based on the evaluation of that one attribute. Suppose the decision-maker does not recognize either Company X or Company Y. In this case, one attribute of the copier may be chosen as the "tie-breaker" in the decision. A second way of breaking the tie would be choose what was done last time, if it worked. Decision-makers will often demonstrate a bias to the status quo. Another less savory method of tie-breaking is to focus on factors not relevant to the decision. For instance, was one salesperson more likeable than the other?

The availability heuristic often leads to the **conjunction fallacy**. Just because we recognize something does not mean the recognition translates into reality. Put another way, a product with a reputation for quality may not in fact be a quality product. It is easy to understand why major corporations spend large amounts of money on both brand and product advertising. Advertising creates brand recognition and awareness, critical factors for those employing either the recognition or availability heuristics to make a decision. Marketing also creates **halo effects**, an overall perception used to "fill in the gaps" when there is a lack of knowledge about particular attributes. In the case of picking out an office copier, all the attributes of the particular copier may not be known, but the brand reputation fills in this lack of knowledge and allows us to make a decision.[25]

A slightly more refined decision process is the **lexicographic heuristic**. A key attribute is selected by the decision-maker and the choice is made based on its evaluation. There is often a hierarchy of attributes in case of a tie among alternatives when evaluating the first attribute. The decision will then be made based on the second key attribute and so on until a clear choice emerges. In our example, suppose the key attribute for the decision-maker is price. If Copier A is less expensive than Copier B, Copier A will be selected. If Copier A and Copier B cost the same, then the next key attribute is examined. Suppose the second key attribute is reliability. If Copier B is more reliable than Copier A the decision-maker will opt for Copier B. Should they be judged equally reliable, the third attribute will be examined. This process will continue until a choice is made.

People use the lexicographic method in their everyday lives. You have decided to go out to dinner and employ a lexicographic rule to choose the restaurant. The most important attribute for you is the size of the portion. Small portions are simply not your thing. If restaurants being considered are judged to provide similar size portions, the next attribute examined is price. If the price of the food is the same at all restaurants, the ambience of each restaurant is then considered. This will continue until an attribute is reached giving one restaurant an advantage.

---

25. Halo effects don't exist only in the business world. Consider what happens in a general election. The voter may be presented with a bewildering array of candidates for many offices, ranging from president down to local town town managers. She may recognize several, but not all of the candidates. The known candidates will often create a halo effect for the other candidates of the same party, giving the voter a reason to choose the entire slate of candidates from that party.

A **semi-lexicographic heuristic** is similar to the lexicographic method but allows decision attributes with similar values to be judged as equals. Suppose the cost of Copier B is only $10 per month more than Copier A. The decision-maker may consider this to be equivalent as the monthly cost differential between the two choices is negligible. Therefore, the next attribute will be considered. The semi-lexicographic method is a compensatory heuristic. A deficiency in one attribute may be overcome by superiority in another attribute. In the copier example, suppose the second decision attribute is reliability. Copier B is judged to be much more reliable than Copier A. The slightly higher monthly cost of Copier B is offset by its greater reliability, making it an acceptable option for the decision-maker. Copier B would be chosen as the new office copier.

One problem with a semi-lexicographic strategy is there might be a violation of the **transitivity principle**. Simply stated, a rational decision-maker preferring option A over B and B over C, would also prefer A over C. However, semi-lexicographic decision making could disrupt that principle. Let's go back to the previous example and amplify it with some additional facts. Suppose Copier A costs $100 per month and requires a high level of service, Copier B $115 per month and requires a low level of service, and Copier C $105 per month requires a medium level of service. If our semi-lexicographic strategy states a ten-dollar price difference per month can be ignored in favor of a lower level of service, an obvious inconsistency occurs. Copier A is preferred to B, and B would be preferred to C, but then C is preferred to A. This is not a trivial situation. One researcher conducted an experiment where his students were shown three potential spouses. None were in any way extreme. The students were shown the potential spouses in pairs. Fully one-quarter of the students were shown to be "irrational" in such situations. The explanation: decisions involving relative strengths and weaknesses of different attributes are hard to compare. In such situations the decision-maker will need to sharpen the decision-rule to eliminate such inconsistencies.

The **elimination by aspects (EBA) heuristic** is an example of a non-compensatory heuristic. Required values for decision attributes are determined and alternatives not meeting the required value for each attribute are dismissed. Suppose the decision-maker requires the copier to function as a scanner and a printer. It must be able to make color copies and can't cost more than a certain amount per month. All copier alternatives that do not meet these criteria are dismissed as untenable. An example of EBA will follow in a subsequent chapter.

## 6.2 Programmed Decision Making

Once the decision has been made, the question of recurrence needs to be addressed. If this decision will need to be made again in the future, consideration should be given to converting the initial decision making into a **programmed decision**.

Programmed decisions are designed to handle recurring issues, often through standard policies and procedures. This ensures consistency of treatment across the organization and across time. It also conserves time as the procedure to follow when dealing with the same or similar decisions is outlined for future decision-makers. Examples of programmed decisions are corporate policy manuals and Internal Revenue Service audit guides. They instruct the decision-makers to follow the same process and make the same decision for similar situations. Complex and novel situations decisions will result in **nonprogrammed decisions** since they often have greater risk and return associated with them.

---

# Chapter Summary

◆ Some decisions result in a small return and entail small risk. These decisions do not require extensive analysis as the cost of analysis could exceed potential benefits of making the decision.

◆ Heuristics are fast and economical ways of making these decisions and often employ "rules of thumb". They are often grounded in the knowledge and background of the decision-maker. Heuristics are not appropriate for decisions involving great risk or great return.

◆ Heuristic decision making often results in programmed decision making. Programmed decision making is often evidenced by highly developed policies and procedures and is also an economical way to conserve organization time and energy when making decisions.

◆ Complex decisions involving high risk and return should be nonprogrammed decisions involving more sophisticated decision analysis methodologies.

# Discussion Questions

1. What is your personal style of decision making? What heuristic do you use most often?

2. Describe one successful decision you had to make recently using a heuristic method. Describe the heuristic method you used. Can you draw a decision tree to describe your decision process?

3. Describe one unsuccessful decision you made recently using a heuristic rule. Describe the heuristic method you used. Why was the decision unsuccessful? Did you apply an incorrect heuristic? Did you properly identify all of the decision attributes before you began the analysis?

---

*Solutions to the above questions can be downloaded from the* **Online Resources** *section of this book on* **www.vibrantpublishers.com**

*This page is intentionally left blank*

# Chapter 7

# Probability and Base Rate Neglect

How do we deal with risk in our decision analyses? This chapter describes how probability theory can be used to analyze risks. It also talks about base rate neglect, a major fallacy in statistical reasoning we often fall into, and Bayes Theorem, a way to take new information into account when we mare making decisions.

Several years ago, a movie named The Minority Report told the story of three psychics who were so good at predicting future murders the perpetrators could be arrested even before they could commit the crime. The psychics were alleged to have a 100% perfect record in predicting these events so there was absolute certainty the perpetrator would commit the crime. Therefore, their arrest was justified. It is only later we learn there were cases when one of the psychics would disagree and a minority report would be returned. These minority reports were suppressed in order to present the illusion of certainty. The fact there could be a minority report introduced probability into the decision making process.

The alleged certainty provided by the psychics and the comfort that came with it disappeared. The system of using psychics could no longer be used by law-enforcement as the future certainty of the crime vanished with the minority report.

We wish we could have absolute certainty about the success of our decisions. Unfortunately, without psychic powers we are unsure of how our decisions will turn out. Our decisions exist in the world of **probability** (risk) and uncertainty.

The probability of an event occurring is represented by a range from zero to one. A probability of 1 indicates complete certainty the event will occur. A probability of 0 indicates it is impossible for the event to occur. The range of numbers in between indicate the probability of the event occurring. We often hear probability being used in our daily lives, captured with such statements such "there is a fifty/fifty chance of rain" or in baseball "his batting average is .250" (the batter successfully achieves first base or beyond one out of every four times at bat).[26] Sometimes the use of probability is more dramatic. In 2004 Dr. Stephan Unwin used Bayes Theorem (a topic later in this chapter) to calculate the probability of the existence of God to be about 67%, or two out of three occurrences.

There are many decision analysis models using probability today. Sometimes the model being used depends on the profession. We will begin our examination of how probability is used in decision making in two professions: the law and accounting.

---

26. Batting average is just one of many decision making tools used in baseball. This particular statistic has come under attack as being somewhat irrelevant in deciding what the true skill level of a batter is.

# 7.1 The Law

Judges and juries rely heavily on probability when rendering judgments. The United States legal system uses three basic probability states:

**Beyond a reasonable doubt**–The standard used in criminal trials. There is much discussion about what this means, but for our purposes the probability of guilt must be near 1.[27] This is why criminal trials use a jury of twelve people who must be unanimous in finding a verdict of guilty.[28] The underlying foundation for this doctrine is the famous dictum "it is better a hundred guilty persons escape than one innocent suffers."[29] One juror out of twelve voting for an acquittal results in the probability of guilt being 92%, resulting in a "hung jury".[30]

**Clear and convincing**–The occurrence of the event is deemed to be "highly probable". Some writers equate this to a 75% probability of occurrence, but this appears to be more of an informal rule of thumb.[31] The clear and convincing standard has

---

27. Or, as I heard one criminal attorney explain it, the evidence "must exceed three standards deviations from the preponderance of evidence standard." In a normal distribution, the mean plus or minus two standard deviations includes over 95% of the data.

28. The United States Supreme Court reaffirmed this principal in April 2020. Military juries, owing to their unique nature, may convict with a two-thirds majority except in death penalty situations. Military juries therefore can't result in a hung jury.

29. William Blackstone, English jurist and commentator on English law put the ratio at 10:1. Benjamin Franklin later increased the ratio to 100:1.

30. A hung jury does not result in an acquittal. The prosecution can elect to retry the case. The finding of not guilty must also be unanimous.

31. Recall the mean plus or minus one standard deviation includes about 68% of the data in a normal distribution.

several applications in law, including the revocation of certain personal rights. For instance, courts require a clear and convincing standard of proof before a State may revoke parental rights[32] or for revocation of parole.

**Preponderance of evidence**–The standard used in civil court matters. A plaintiff needs to produce the greater weight of evidence the defendant committed some action such as a breach of contract or a tort to achieve a guilty result. Using statistical language, the plaintiff needs to prove there is a greater than 50% chance the defendant committed an action to prevail. This is also sometimes referred to as the **more likely than not**[33] standard.

A famous demonstration of the difference between the "beyond the reasonable doubt" standard and the "preponderance of evidence" standard occurred in the trials of O.J. Simpson, a famous football player. Simpson was accused of the murder of two people. He was acquitted by the jury in the criminal case where the standard was beyond a reasonable doubt but was convicted in the civil case where the lower preponderance of evidence standard prevailed.

At the end of the day a judge or jury does not have to quantify the probability of occurrence. They need only develop a subjective probability exceeding the required threshold.[34]

---

32. Santosky v. Kramer. 4 455 U.S. 745 (1982).

33. The use of the more likely than not standard can be seen in many places. For example, the United States Internal Revenue Service makes use of this term when dealing with uncertain tax positions. U.S. Senator Susan Collins of Maine used this standard to support her decision to vote for the confirmation of Judge Brett Kavanaugh to the United States Supreme Court.

34. Subjective probabilities are utilized when evaluating the probability of an infrequent event. There also may be no empirical data available to the decision-maker to make a more refined estimate.

# 7.2 Accounting for Contingent Liabilities

The accounting profession uses probabilities in many situations but its most critical use is seen in the accounting for contingencies.[35] To assess potential losses, the accounting profession has adopted the **"probable and estimable"** rule of accounting for loss contingencies.[36]

Loss contingencies often result from events occurring in the current period but potentially entailing future period losses. The classic example of a financial accounting contingency is litigation. Suppose your organization has been sued in the last quarter of the year. Complex litigation may take years to reach final resolution. Yet, your organization must publish financial statements in several months, and the legal process is in its very early phases. Discovery hasn't even begun yet. What is the proper accounting, if any?

In such a situation an organization must determine the proper accounting for the litigation at year-end. The first step in the process is to assign a probability to the outcome of the litigation and the potential for loss as follows:

**Remote possibility**–The probability of a potential loss is slight

---

35. The first accounting requirement controlling the accounting for contingencies was Statement of Financial Accounting Standards #5 issued by the Financial Accounting Standards Board ("FASB") in 1975. This is a very "mature" accounting standard and has proved to be very workable. It has since been included in the FASB codification project as ASC 450. The American Bar Association permits attorneys to issue letters to independent certified public accountants discussing litigation contingencies adopting the terminology established in this accounting standard.

36. Accountants follow the principle of conservatism, so gain contingencies are not recognized in financial accounting unless there is verifiable evidence of such an event (e.g. unrealized gains of investment securities with a wide market. ) Recording of unrealized gains is therefore very rare in American accounting.

or negligible. In the litigation example, perhaps the organization's attorneys have determined the lawsuit to be frivolous. No loss is recorded and there is no disclosure in the financial statements.

**Reasonably possible**–The probability of a potential loss is greater than remote, but less than likely. Suppose your attorney has informed you there is a one in four chance your organization will lose the lawsuit and will be required to make a large payment to the plaintiff. At this point, no loss is accrued, but stakeholders of the organization would certainly want to know there is the risk of a large potential loss. Accounting rules require the disclosure of the lawsuit but no loss accrual.

**Probable**–The future loss is likely to occur. Suppose this is not the first time your organization has been sued over this particular issue and it has lost or settled several of these lawsuits. This indicates a high probability at least some loss will be incurred in this lawsuit. Therefore, an anticipated loss will be recorded[37] and appropriate disclosure will be made in the financial statements.

Is the organization done after this initial assessment? No. The probability and estimation of the loss must be reviewed every accounting period until the contingency is resolved to determine if there has been any change. The potential loss and disclosures are adjusted accordingly in the year of the change of circumstances. In many cases the probability estimates are subjective. More rigorous

---

37. This presumes the amount of the loss or at least a range of loss estimates can be reliably estimated. If a reliable estimate of the loss can't be made, only disclosure is required. If a range of loss can be estimated, the low point of the range is accrued unless one point in the range has a greater probability of occurring than the others. The assumption of an equal probability of each potential outcome in the range unless there is evidence to the contrary is known as the Laplace Principle in decision analysis. Simulation techniques can be quite useful in this exercise, as we will see in a future chapter.

decision analysis tools such as simulations can assist accountants in quantifying the probability of a loss and the estimate of loss ranges more precisely.

Taxing authorities have a different idea about what constitutes "probable and estimable". Obviously, a loss accrual results in an additional deduction on a tax return and lower taxes due. In the case of litigation, the organization might be required to record a financial accounting expense even before it even steps into the courthouse. However, this will not be deductible on its tax return. In the United States, a deduction must satisfy the **all events** test. This requires a liability to become fixed and the amount determinable prior being deductible.

Let's compare the all events test to the financial accounting for contingencies. Suppose an organization is subject to a lawsuit where its attorney believes a loss is almost certain to occur, and the attorney can reasonably estimate the amount of the loss. Perhaps there has been a string of lawsuits for product liability that have been recently settled, so the attorney has a good basis to make an estimate. At the end of the fiscal period the organization must recognize a loss in its financial statements. However, this financial accounting loss is not deductible for tax purposes until a settlement occurs or a trial fixes the amount of the liability. At that point the organization can accrue the litigation loss for tax purposes even though it has not paid the settlement. The liability has passed the all events test and is considered a valid deduction.

# 7.3 Using Probability in Decision Making

In the above examples, the probability estimates can be subjective probabilities, vaguely quantifiable because the probable outcomes exceed a required threshold. Suppose we want to quantify probabilities to sharpen our decision making processes. Let's begin with a review of probability theory.

Besides subjective probability estimation, there are two other ways probability is estimated: the **classical probability** method and the **relative frequency** method. In classical probability, each possible state has an equal chance of occurring. When flipping a coin there is a 50% chance of getting heads or tail. Either has an equal chance of happening barring the near impossible state of the coin landing on its side.[38] Similarly, the probability of rolling a five on a die is one out of six or approximately 16.7%.

Relative frequency probability is more experiential in nature. The probability of an event is calculated as the number of times the event occurs out of the total number of possible events. For example, unlike the rolling of dice, a baseball player's batting average is calculated as the number of times he or she safely reaches first base out of the total number of at bats (opportunities).[39] In most cases, relative frequency probability is what we are dealing with in the business world. A weakness of relative frequency probability is its dependency on the number of

---

38. This possibility, as remote as it is, demonstrates that in even such a simple situation there is some uncertainty, as remote as this possibility is. This is one of the basic principles behind scenario planning, discussed elsewhere in this book.

39. For the baseball purist, this number is adjusted for the number of walks and errors. The weakness of using batting average as a barometer of a players' skill lead in part to the rise of sabermetrics in baseball and other sports.

trials. Flipping a coin and achieving heads two out of three times results in a probability of approximately 67%. Flipping the same coin, a thousand times will yield a probability of that occurring about 50% of the time. Decision-makers need to be concerned about sample size since extreme values are more likely to occur with small sample sizes than with larger sample sizes. Given our cognitive limitations, it is very easy for a decision-maker to draw an incorrect inference from the results of a small sample.

**Mutually exclusive events** are also known as **disjoint events**. Two or more events are mutually exclusive if the occurrence of one event prevents the simultaneous occurrence of another event. The flipping of a coin results in mutually exclusivity. The result is either heads or tails but can't be both. The rolling of a die has a same result. You either roll a five or you don't. If two events are mutually exclusive, the probability of either of them happening is the sum of the two probabilities. Using standard notation, the probability of mutually exclusive events A or B is:

$$P(A \text{ or } B) = P(A) + P(B)$$

The probability of either heads or tails is 100%. The probability of rolling a one or a six is approximately 33.34%, or 1 out of three chances.

If events A and B are not mutually exclusive, the probability of A or B occurring is the sum of the individual probabilities of A and B occurring less the probability of both of then occurring. This eliminates the possibility of double counting when both A and B occur. Putting this into notation, we see:

$$P(A \text{ or } B) = P(A) + P(B) - P(A \text{ and } B)$$

Suppose you want to calculate the odds of rolling an even number on a die or a number greater than four. The outcome set $S_1$ = the possible outcomes of rolling an even number = {2,4,6}. The outcome set $S_2$ = the possible outcomes of rolling a number greater than four = {5,6}. Rolling a six can occur in each outcome set that must be accounted for. This is defined as $P(S_1 + S_2)$. Therefore, $P(S_1)$ = .5, $P(S_2)$ = .333, and $P(S_1 + S_2)$ = .167. Using our formula, the probability of rolling an even number or a number greater than four is approximately .67, or two out of three chances. We can confirm the mathematics by observing after we eliminate the double-counting of the number six, our final solution set is S = {2,4,5,6} or four of six possibilities.

Complementary events occur when there are only two outcomes. The probability of getting heads on a coin flip is 50%. The complement, flipping tails, is 50% as well. A baseball player's batting average is .310. The complement to that is .690, or the number of times a player does not safely reach base. The player either gets a base hit or doesn't. The probability of event A not occurring can be expressed as:

$$P(not\ A) = 1 - P(A)$$

Alternatively, it can be written as:

$$P(A') = 1 - P(A)$$

**Marginal probability** is the probability of an event occurring regardless of the outcome of another event. For instance, if the flip of a coin is truly random, the marginal probability of getting heads is .5. Despite the belief of many, the outcome of certain events does not impact the outcome of subsequent events. This is known at the gambler's fallacy. Many gamblers believe a string of random events will make other events more likely. For instance, flipping heads four tosses in a row doesn't make tails more likely on the fifth flip. Prior flips of a coin don't impact successive flips of the coins. Lottery players will often continue to play the same number time and time again because it is "due to come up". Unfortunately, previous numbers drawn in the lottery don't impact future drawings.

**Conditional probability** is the probability of one event occurring depending on the outcome of another event. An example of conditional probability is estimating the probability you have the flu if you have a sore throat and sniffles.

If events A and B are **independent events** the probability of A happening has nothing to do with B happening and vice versa. The probability of A happening given B occurred is still the probability of A happening. By the same token, the probability of B happening given A occurred is the probability of B happening. This can be notated as:

$$P(A \mid B) = P(A) \text{ and } P(B \mid A) = P(B)$$

If A and B are independent events, the probability of both A and B occurring is the product of the two possibilities. The probability of rolling two sixes on two dice is one out of 36, or one-sixth times one sixth. This notation is:

$$P(A \text{ and } B) = P(A) \times P(B)$$

If A and B are not independent events and the probability of event B is dependent on event A occurring, the probability of A and B occurring is the product of the probability of A occurring and the probability of B occurring given A has occurred. The notation for this is:

$$P(A \text{ and } B) = P(A) \times P(B \mid A)$$

We have seen the probability of rolling two sixes on two dice is one out of 36. However, if we know that first roll of the die is a six, then:

$$P(6,6) = 1 \times .167 = .167$$

This probability is substantially higher than that of rolling two sixes on two dice.

Suppose a baseball player has a batting average of .300. This means he will get a base hit three out of ten times at bat. Suppose he also will attempt to steal second base (move from first to second base while the next pitch is being delivered) every time he reaches first base. He is thrown out fifty percent of the time and reaches second fifty percent of the time. In this case, P1 = P(base hit) = .3. The player can't attempt to steal second base without safely reaching first base. The probability of safely reaching second base, P2 = .5. Therefore, P(A and B) = .15. Interpreting this data, the batter will either be on second base at the end of two plays 15% of the time or he will not be on base at all. Seventy percent of the time he will not safely reach first base. When he does, he is thrown out attempting to steal second base half the time, resulting in the 15% probability of being on second base at the end of two plays.

Assume the same facts as in the previous example, but now include another condition. The batter will only attempt to steal second base 50% of the time. It is easy to see that:

$$P(A \text{ and } B \text{ and } C) = P(A) \times P(B \mid A) \times P(C \mid A).$$

In this case, there are three possible outcomes after two successive plays. There is a 7.5% chance the batter will be on second base, a 15% chance he will be on first base, and a 77.5% chance he will not be on base at all. Even these simplistic examples demonstrate a chain of probability computations can become quite complex. A probability tree is a graphical way to portray the potential outcomes of such events. It accounts for all possible outcomes.

What is the probability of drawing two diamonds from a deck of cards in successive draws, assuming replacement of the first card into the deck? The probability of drawing one diamond from a deck of cards is 25% (Event A). Putting the card back into the deck and drawing again results in another 25% chance of drawing a diamond. Hence, the probability of drawing two successive diamonds is one out of 16, or 25% times 25%. A probability tree is used to graphically demonstrate this:

**Figure 7.1**

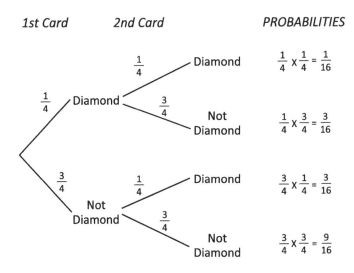

1st Card          2nd Card                    PROBABILITIES

$\frac{1}{4}$ Diamond $\frac{1}{4}$ Diamond $\frac{1}{4} \times \frac{1}{4} = \frac{1}{16}$

$\frac{3}{4}$ Not Diamond $\frac{1}{4} \times \frac{3}{4} = \frac{3}{16}$

$\frac{3}{4}$ Not Diamond $\frac{1}{4}$ Diamond $\frac{3}{4} \times \frac{1}{4} = \frac{3}{16}$

$\frac{3}{4}$ Not Diamond $\frac{3}{4} \times \frac{3}{4} = \frac{9}{16}$

Notice all possibilities are accounted for by the probability tree.

A probability distribution describes all the possible values in a given range and the probability that each can occur. A discrete probability function can only have integers as its outcomes. In many business situations, the solution set will consist of positive integers. For instance, it is not possible for an airline to fly 1.5 airplanes to a selected destination. It can fly one or two airplanes, but not 1.5. The graph of a discrete probability function has integers on the x axis and the probability of each event on the y axis as follows:

**Figure 7.2**

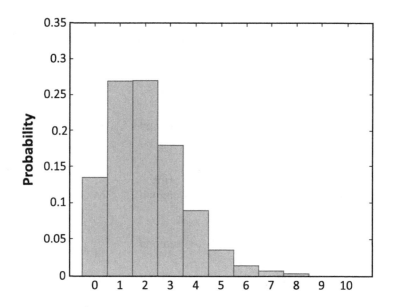

A **continuous probability function** may have numbers other than integers in its range. One such function is the normal distribution, or the familiar "bell curve." In the following diagram, we see a standard distribution with a range of possible outcomes from 5 to 16 and any fractional number in between. The total area under the curve is 1, or 100%. The area encompasses all possible outcomes of the function.

**Figure 7.3**

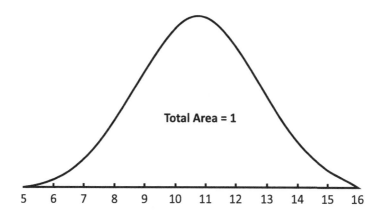

Total Area = 1

5  6  7  8  9  10  11  12  13  14  15  16

This Photo by Unknown Author is licensed under CC BY

# 7.4 Expected Value

The **expected monetary value** of a function is the total of each possible outcome multiplied by the probability of its occurrence. It is the mean or average expected result. The actual result can be above or below the expected mean, resulting in risk. Assuming the probability of an outcome $x_n$ is $P_n$, the general formula for the expected monetary value of a function is:

$$E(x) = P_1x_1 + P_2x_2 + \ldots + P_ix_i$$

All things being equal, the decision-maker should choose the option generating the highest expected value. Let's assume there is a decision you will make. The probability of the decision being a success is 50%, in which case the profit will be $300. If the decision ends up being a failure, the loss will be $100. The expected monetary value of this function is $100, or (50%) x ($300) less (50%) x ($100). If asked, a rational decision-maker should decide to accept this bet since it has a positive expected value. However, time and time again, otherwise seemingly rational decision-makers declined, opting out of the game.[40] Why?

A major deficiency of the expected value methodology is it only considers return, but not risk.[41] Expected value assumes the decision-maker is neutral to risk. However, we have seen from prospect theory the reference point of the decision-maker impacts the decision. Decision-makers tend to be risk-averse. This is even more pronounced if the potential loss may cause serious damage or even bankrupt the company. The decision-maker may decide the risk of the negative outcome is too severe to contemplate and pass on the opportunity.

The decision-maker also understands this decision is a one-time event with a real possibility of failure. However, if you

---

40. This is a variation of the famous Samuelson bet. Paul Samuelson, the winner of the Nobel Prize in Economics in 1970, demonstrated more people would take the bet if you ran the trial one hundred times. They instinctively knew about odds in the long run.

41. Risk is measured with probability and measures of dispersion such as the variance and standard deviation. As a reminder, the standard deviation is the square root of the variance. Therefore, the standard deviation can never be negative. One way to measure risk is by using the **coefficient of variation**, or the expected value divided by the standard deviation. Students of finance will recognize this as the basis of the **Sharpe ratio**, the computation of the excess return of a stock. The Sharpe ratio is the expected return on the stock minus the risk-free rate of return, all divided by the standard deviation of the stock returns.

change the parameters of the decision to say there will be many repetitions of the event, and any early potential losses could be absorbed by the company, decision-makers would be much more prone to making the decision and accepting the gamble.

Expected value uses a **symmetric measure of risk**. Both positive and negative variances are included in the computation of variance and therefore, risk. Yet, is that how we truly view risk? A pleasant surprise to the upside (a positive variance) is often not considered risk. It is considered good fortune! Consequently, some stock brokerage firms will only calculate variance and standard deviation on days a stock has closed down, regarding this as the best measure of risk exposure.

Another deficiency of the expected monetary value approach is it only considers one attribute: monetary values. Instead of maximizing profit, many decision-makers seek to maximize utility. Let's examine this aspect of decision making with some examples. People go to casinos and gamble even though they know they will generally lose. There is a whole industry built on this proposition. So, why do people gamble? Unless having a gambling addiction, the occasional gambler will find going to the casino entertaining, increasing overall utility to the consumer. They accept a certain amount of loss as a price to pay for entertainment. If you throw in the possibility of hitting the jackpot, you have really caught people's attention.

Earlier in my career I worked for a privately-owned company having a substantial amount of cash. As a diligent financial officer, I asked the owners if I should invest the company funds during the time of the year when they were not needed. I was confident I could improve the overall net income of the company by investing these otherwise idle assets. This obvious course of action (at least I thought so!) was not met with a great deal of enthusiasm by the owners. In their mental accounting, the money was their retirement fund, and they wanted to avoid all investment risk no matter how slight. The owners were motivated by safety and not return. Their utility was maximized by knowing their funds were safe. In other words, they did not want to talk about the return on the funds, but the return of the funds. After some discussion, I did convince them to allow some investment, but their risk aversion limited the choice of investments. As the stock market has inherent risks, I decided the best choice of investments was U.S. Treasury securities and mortgage-backed debt. Both seemed to meet the safety criterion at that time. I left the company before the economic troubles of 2008 and have long wondered what would have happened if I had invested the company funds into the mortgage backed securities market when the sub-prime mortgage crisis was occurring.

A common representation of a utility function is a graph such as this:

**Figure 7.4**

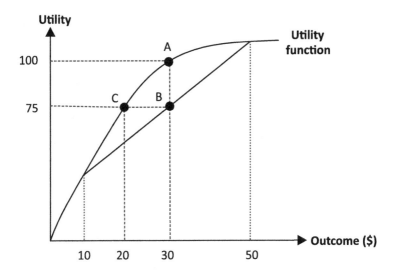

The shape of the utility function reveals the attitude towards risk. A concave utility function implies risk-aversion. In the above graph, no more utility is generated after $50 of return. Consequently, only sufficient risk required to generate $50 of outcome should be incurred. A convex utility function implies risk-seeking, as utility only rises perceptibly after a large increase in expected value. A risk neutral utility function would be represented by a line with a forty-five-degree angle from the origin.

While it is often not practical to use utility functions, intuitively understanding the shape and slope of not only your utility function but of those you are dealing with can be critical to the success of a decision. In the example I gave above, the owners' utility curve was extremely concave. If I had thought about that for a moment, I may not have come to them with such an ambitious investment plan.

## 7.5 Decision Trees

One way to effectively present expected values is through the use of a **decision tree**. A decision tree is a graphical representation of all possible outcomes of an event and their probability of occurring. Decision trees are read backwards that is, they are "rolled back" to understand their meaning.

**Figure 7.5**

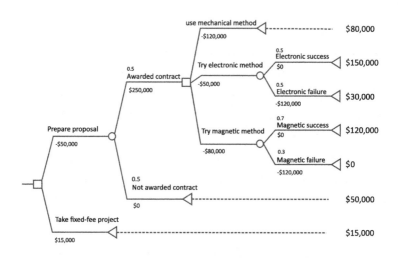

The above decision tree calculates the expected monetary value of the successful sale of a manufacturing process. The decision-maker is faced with the question of whether she should bid on the contract for all of the work, which will cost $50,000, or simply accept a portion of the work for a fixed fee, resulting in net income of $15,000. She estimates the probability of winning the entire contract at 50%, and there are three possible methods of completing the required work. In this case, the highest possible return is $150,000 by using the electrical method. How this is achieved and the probability of achieving that return is calculated by "rolling back the tree" from that endpoint.

The expected value of bidding is calculated as follows:

**Table 7.1**

|          |                         | **Probability** | **Value**  | **E(V)**   |
|----------|-------------------------|-----------------|------------|------------|
| **Win Bid** | Electrical successful   | .25             | $150,000   | $37,500    |
| **Win Bid** | Electrical unsuccessful | .25             | 30,000     | 7,500      |
| **Loss Bid** |                        | .50             | -50,000    | - 25,000   |
| **Total**   |                         | 1.0             |            | $25,000    |

The total expected value of the entire project after bidding, winning, and using the electronic process is $10,000 more compared to the value of accepting only part of the work. Should the decision-maker then bid for the project? That will depend entirely on other decision factors. Not bidding could free up resources to do other work. The opportunity cost of preparing the bid could be very high. The decision-maker may also be risk averse and decide the risk of being out $50,000 (preparing the bid and losing, a 50% chance) is simply too high to contemplate. Even though bidding has a higher expected value than the accepting only a piece of the work, the contractor could rationally decide to pass on this project. Losing the project would just create too much pain and disutility.

# 7.6 Bayesian Inference

When we think of statistics, we most often think of using the relative frequency approach to statistics. We draw a random sample from a large population and apply various statistical processes to that sample to come up with such useful information as the mean and the standard deviation. If we have the time and resources, we could pick an even larger sample to increase the reliability of our estimates. With the relative frequency approach, the more data the better. However, this can be a very costly and take a great deal of time, both of which are generally in short supply in most organizations.

Bayesian statistics is another less costly approach to statistics and has some significant advantages. **Bayes Theorem** is a profound statistical insight that has been called the cornerstone of rational thought.[42] Thomas Bayes was an eighteenth-century Presbyterian minister who dabbled in statistics. Bayes Theorem comes to us partly by chance,[43] as he did not publish his findings during his lifetime.

---

42. The claim is extreme, but it is certainly directionally correct.

43. An irony Bayes himself, as a statistician might appreciate.

Bayes Theorem is generally notated as:

**Figure 7.6**

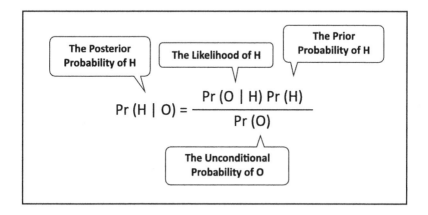

This Photo by Unknown Author is licensed under CC BY-NC-ND

### The Posterior Probability of H
The probability of a hypothesis (H) given an observation (O). This represents your updated degree of belief.

### The Likelihood of H
The probability of an observation given a hypothesis. In other words, the probability that the hypothesis confers upon the observation.

### The Prior Probability of H
The probability of a hypothesis (H) before the observation. (Not necessarily a priori concept, can sometimes be based on previous empirical evidence}

## The Unconditional Probability of O

The probability of an observation irrespective of any particular hypothesis. Can occasionally be restated as:

**Pr (O⏐H) Pr (H) + Pr (O⏐~H) Pr (~H)**

In other words the unconditional probability of O is represented by the likelihood of H times the prior probability of H, plus the likelihood of not H times the prior probability of not H. This restatement is often useful in the case of a test with a known rate of false positive and false negatives.

We often know something about the population we are studying. Perhaps this information is a good estimate of what the probabilities of each potential outcome is or the population mean. This is where Bayes Theorem comes in. It provides a method for us to update our information about the population.

Let's see how Bayes Theorem is applied in a baseball situation. we know what the lifetime batting average of a major league baseball player is. This is known as the **prior probability** or Pr(H) in the above diagram. Suppose the player has been on a hitting streak. What is the probability he will continue this streak the next time he is at bat? We are searching for the **posterior probability**, our updated estimate based on new data (the hitting streak). This is denoted as Pr(H⏐O) in the above diagram. The new data, or the likelihoods, modifies the prior possibility to come up with a new posterior probability.

Let's continue with a baseball example again. Player K on your favorite team has a batting average of .250, making him a very average player. He has played for your team for several seasons, so he has been at bat about 1,000 times in previous seasons. Of those 1,000 times, he has reached base safely 250 times, meaning he has not reached base 750 times. This year he has been up to bat 100 times and has reached base 35 times, for a batting average this season of .350. What can you expect form this player for the rest of the season? How do you take this information into account? How do you update your knowledge about this player? Should you?

The answer is you can rationally do this with Bayes Theorem because you have a prior probability. You expect the player to be average, but he is outperforming your expectations in the early part of the season. Applying Bayes Theorem, you add the new amount of base hits to the numerator and the new amount of at bats to the denominator and take their ratio. The new batting average (the posterior probability) is computed as 285/1,100 or .259, still very average. In other words, you don't expect the player to continue his torrid pace for the rest of the year since he is still an average player despite the latest streak.[44] He might completely surprise you and do so, but it is highly unlikely that will be the case. You expect a **regression to the mean**.[45] Notice a Bayesian statistician has a lower batting average estimate (.269) then the frequentist statistician (.350) and is probably more reliable, given what you know about this player.

The regression to the mean is not only important in sports decisions. Take investment advisors for instance. They often advertise the above average returns they earn for investors, but none have been able to continue this performance over the long-haul. They were not able to replicate their results on a consistent basis over time. This stands to reason since any method they have used to secure superior returns will soon be copied

---

44. Numerous factors go into this assessment. The player may become fatigued over a long season. Major League Baseball teams in the United States play 162 games per year. The player may get injured, reducing his performance over time. As he ages, his skills may begin to erode. Of course, the degradation in performance can also be analyzed through the use of Big Data.

45. That is why you don't see any .400 hitters anymore!

by competitors, who will also begin achieving these results. When you couple this with the efficient market hypothesis (all information about the stock has already been factored into its price, even educated guesses about investment returns and stock prices begin to look more and more like sheer guesswork.

Bayesian statistics does have its detractors. For instance, having different prior probabilities impacts the posterior probability. Having varying amounts of information in forming the prior probability also impacts the posterior probability even if the prior probabilities are the same. Continuing the baseball example, three players have the exact same batting average, but with differing numbers of base hits and times at bat comprising their prior probability. All of them are hitting .250, but Player L has hit safely 25 out of a hundred times, Player M 50 times out of 200, and Player N 125 times out of 500. They all then reach base safely 35 times out there next 100 times at bat. What are their Bayesian batting averages? Player L is hitting .300 [60/200], Player M .283 [85/300], and Player N .267 [160/600]. The fact Player K has lit up the baseball stadium with his batting pyrotechnics the last hundred times at bat is of much less import than for Players L and M, who have been doing just as well but with much fewer times at bat. Again, the statistics should not control the decision about which player to put on the field that day, but it should be factored into that decision.

**Table 7.2**

|   | Prior Hits | Prior AB | Prior Avg | Likely Hits | Likely AB | Likely Avg | Pstr.Pr Hits | Pstr.Pr AB | Pstr.Pr Avg |
|---|---|---|---|---|---|---|---|---|---|
| **K** | 250 | 1,000 | .250 | 35 | 100 | .350 | 285 | 1,100 | .259 |
| **L** | 25 | 100 | .250 | 35 | 100 | .350 | 60 | 200 | .300 |
| **M** | 50 | 200 | .250 | 35 | 100 | .350 | 85 | 300 | .283 |
| **N** | 125 | 500 | .250 | 35 | 100 | .350 | 160 | 600 | .267 |

In reality, the actual statistics available to a manager about Player K can be overwhelming precisely because Player K has been at bat so many times in his career. The manager will not only know Player K's overall batting average, but also his averages against left-handed versus right-handed pitchers, in day games versus night games, against the particular pitchers he will face that day, etc. Big Data can be sliced and diced many ways. As we have seen, some of the information is meaningful and some of it not. In the end, it may be the newer players L and M the manager perceives as the true challenge (risk) since he has less data about them.

This type of analysis has also been applied to basketball. There are numerous articles applying Bayesian statistics to the "hot hand". Suppose a player has had an 50% shooting percentage from the floor, and now makes ten baskets in a row. He or she obviously has the "hot hand". Will this continue? Although there have been articles of late suggesting this is the case, the straight application of Bayesian statistics would suggest that is not the case.[46]

---

46. Amos Tversky was an avid basketball fan and did some of the first work in this field. The recent research centers not around the shooter, but how the defense reacts to the shooter and other factors.

Bayes Theorem has implications not just for sports but also for business, the law, and everyday life. Assume a patient tests positive for cancer. One can only imagine the horror the patient feels when the doctor says that, but is a positive test result the end of the story?

Let's imagine the following facts:

$P(A)$ = the probability a certain type of cancer occurs in the population. In this case, let's suppose it is 1%.

$P(B)$ = The Chance of a positive result on a test. The test will return a true positive 90% of the time. In other words, it will result in a false negative of 10% of the time.[47]

We are searching for P(cancer, positive), or the probability there is cancer and a positive test result. Using Bayes formula, we must therefore solve:

$$\frac{P(positive \mid cancer) \times P(cancer)}{P(positive)}$$

Substituting all of our knowns for the terms, we arrive at:

$$\frac{(.90)(.01)}{(.009) + (.099)}$$

or, roughly 9%. Therefore, a patient testing positive for this type of cancer will in reality not have a 90% chance of having this disease, but about a 9% chance. This is a significant difference from the perceived probability of the original test results.

---

47. For the purposes of simplicity, the fact a false positive is much better than a false negative is not factored into this discussion.

Using actual numbers will further illustrate this. Using the same information given in this example, let's take a sample of one thousand people tested for cancer. We know only 1%, or ten of the people will have cancer. This leaves 990 who do not have cancer. The test will falsely identify ten percent of this population with having cancer, or 99 people. In total then, the test will identify 109 people (the ten that actually do have cancer plus the 99 false positives) out of the thousand as having cancer. However, only 10 people of that 109 will have cancer, or again approximately 9%. They may have renewed hope, there is no cancer.[48]

Why do we then tend to accept the results of the test so quickly? The human mind homes in on specific numbers much more easily than it comprehends larger general statistics, especially when there is time-pressure involved. Ignoring the larger rate of occurrence in the population is called **base rate neglect** or the **base rate fallacy**. Our minds simply pass over this information to the detriment of the decision. When there is no better estimate of probability, the prior probability should be utilized as the anchor for decision analysis. This also holds true when the quality of the new information is suspect. Unfortunately, since we can become fixated on more specific data, we tend to reject the base rate and focus on that data, even if it is not particularly informative or even correct.

48. Don Redelmeier MD is quoted by Michael Lewis in his book The Undoing Project as saying: "In math you always check your work. In medicine, no." This speaks anecdotally about a lack of control and process in the medical profession.

# Chapter Summary

◆ Probability theory can be used to manage risk.

◆ The expected monetary value of an event is the sum of each potential outcome times the probability of the outcome.

◆ Expected value is one important decision factor in making a decision with quantifiable attributes. However, it does not take into account the risk-aversion of the decision-maker or their utility.

◆ Bayesian statistics gives the decision-maker a blueprint for taking into account new information about a population.

◆ Bayesian inference begins with the prior probability. This is updated by the likelihood, resulting in the posterior probability.

◆ We are often drawn to the more specific statistic when we are dealing with a population. We tend to ignore the prior probability, resulting in the base rate fallacy.

# Discussion Questions

The following problems were drawn from the research of Kahneman and Tversky:

1. A lily pad is growing in a local pond. It doubles every day. At the end of ten days the pond is completely covered. How many days did it take to cover one-half of the pond?

2. Linda is 31 years old, single, outspoken and very bright. She majored in philosophy in college. As a student, she was deeply concerned with issues of discrimination and social justice, and also participated in anti-nuclear demonstrations. Which of the following is more likely?

   a. Linda is a bank teller

   b. Linda is a bank teller and is active in the feminist movement.

3. Two cab companies operate in a city, the Green and Blue Cabs. 85% of the cabs are green and 15% are Blue. A cab is involved in an accident. A witness identified the cab as Blue. The judge hearing the case concluded the witness could correctly identify each of the colors 80% of the time and failed the other 20%. What is the probability a Blue Cab was involved in the accident rather than a Green Cab?

4. 3% of college students are computer science majors. You meet a student who you believe is four times more likely to be a computer science major than other students. What is the probability he is a computer science major?

# Test Your Knowledge

1. What is the probability of drawing two jacks from a standard deck of cards if the first card drawn is replaced after the first draw?

2. What is the probability of drawing two jacks from a standard deck of cards if the first card drawn is a jack and is NOT replaced after the first draw?

3. What is the probability of drawing two jacks from a standard deck of cards if the first card drawn is a NOT a jack and is NOT replaced after the first draw?

4. What is the probability of having two girls as children?

5. What is the probability of having two girls given the first child was a girl?

6. What is the probability of rolling a six on two dice?

7. Revise the probability tree for drawing two diamonds from a deck of cards if there is no replacement.

---

*Solutions to the above questions can be downloaded from*
*the* **Online Resources** *section of this book on*
**www.vibrantpublishers.com**

# Chapter **8**

# The SMART Method

M any decisions we face have both qualitative and quantitative attributes. How should a decision-maker balance them? The SMART method covered in this chapter is one way to do that!

## 8.1 Using the SMART Method

Some of the most difficult but yet common decisions we make involves both quantitative and qualitative data. We seem to be more comfortable dealing with quantitative data when making decisions. We pull statistics and mathematics out of our toolbox to deal with quantitative data. How do we deal with the inclusion of qualitative data in the decision making process? Fortunately, there are several methods that allow the decision-maker to do just that. These are known as **Weighted Attribute Decision Methods (WADM)**. In general terms WADM uses a weighting scheme to determine the importance of each decision attribute. They are especially useful when there is a large number of complex alternatives and decision attributes. The first such method we will consider is the **Simple Multi-Attribute Rating Technique**, also known as **SMART**. Let's look at a few examples of how SMART works.

Baseball is big business in many countries around the world, particularly in the United States. There are thirty major league baseball teams and innumerable minor league, college, and high school teams. For decades baseball decisions were made "off the cuff" and by experiential knowledge. Heuristics were often used by general managers and managers in key situations. For example, many managers began to notice right-handed batters did better against left-handed pitchers, and the baseball platoon system was born. If a team was playing against a left-handed pitcher that day the managers would put as many right-handed batters into the line-up as possible.

That began to change near the end of the last century. A revolution in baseball statistics occurred, spurred on by Bill James and the Society of American Baseball Researchers. The old management methods began to fade away and a new data driven methodology called **sabermetrics** (a portmanteau of the acronym for the Society of Baseball Researchers and metrics) quickly began to gain ground. Currently, all major league baseball teams employ some form of sabermetrics. We will use an extremely simplified example of baseball analysis to demonstrate the SMART method.

Three of the most commonly quoted statistics for batters[49] in baseball are:

- **Batting Average (BA)**–the number of times a batter safely reaches first base through his own efforts. BA is quoted as a percentage of one thousand.[50] So, someone reaching base one out of four times is said to be "batting .250"–spoken as 250. This is considered average for a major league batter.

- **Home runs (HR)**–the number of times a batter hits the ball out of the ballpark. This counts as one run. It is one of the most dramatic plays in baseball and fans love it. Unfortunately, such power hitters often do not have a high batting average as their "swing for the fences" style of batting results in many strikeouts.

- **Runs Batted In (RBI)**–the number of times a batter hits the ball and runners on base score at least one run. It is thought to be an indication of how well a player responds in a pressure situation.

These three statistics are all indicators of performance but have different units of measurement. Batting average is a percentage, while home runs and runs batted in are integers. At least two of the statistics are inversely related. The greater the number of home runs, the lower the batting average generally is.[51] Baseball teams also value other attributes of players, such as their leadership skills and work ethic. These intangible skills are qualitative

---

49. Pitchers, who comprise half the team, are measured with other statistics such as the won-loss records and earned run average.

50. An everyday player may come up to bat five hundred or even six hundred times in one season.

51. This is not always the case. The baseball Triple Crown is awarded to someone who leads the league in all three categories. This has only happened twelve times since 1920.

rather than quantitative.

Finally, baseball is a business. Players are paid salaries. Their contracts cost the team millions of dollars per year and can run for many years. A major league team roster has forty players. Its total payroll can be hundreds of million dollars. Given the variety of data and player attributes, how can a team decide which players to choose for its roster?

Suppose a team has the choice of adding one player out of four possible candidates. The salient information about the players are as follows:

**Table 8.1**

| | **Batting Average** | **Home Runs** | **Runs Batted In** | **Salary (in mil)** | **Intangibles** |
|---|---|---|---|---|---|
| | **Raw Statistics** | | | | |
| **Player A** | 0.251 | 50 | 80 | 25 | 7 |
| **Player B** | 0.272 | 40 | 90 | 20 | 8 |
| **Player C** | 0.293 | 30 | 100 | 15 | 9 |
| **Player D** | 0.313 | 20 | 70 | 10 | 10 |

The tricky part will be how the team factors in the intangible attributes a player brings to the team. The manager was asked to score the four players on a scale of one to ten for the intangible attributes with ten being given to the best performer and the other three players being judged against that player.

The next step is to provide weights for the various attributes and rank the players by each attribute in a similar way the intangible aspects were weighted. For instance, the player with the most home runs was given a ten for that decision factor and the other players were scored in relation to the first player.

The introduction of weights can have the advantage or reducing the number of decision factors. As the number of factors increase the weights become smaller and smaller. At a certain point these minor factors can be left out of a decision without fear of committing major error. Should the eventual evaluation be extremely close, the SMART model can be rerun with the additional factors.

In the case we are examining, the weighting and the ranking are as follows:

**Table 8.2**

| | Ranking and Weights | | | | | |
|---|---|---|---|---|---|---|
| | Batting Average | Home Runs | Runs Batted In | Salary (in mil) | Intangibles | Total |
| Weights | 20% | 20% | 10% | 40% | 10% | 100% |
| Player A | 4 | 10 | 8 | 4 | 7 | |
| Player B | 6 | 8 | 9 | 6 | 8 | |
| Player C | 8 | 6 | 10 | 8 | 9 | |
| Player D | 10 | 4 | 7 | 10 | 10 | |

Management was facing budget pressure, so it assigned the highest weight (40%) to the salary factor. Therefore, the less the player was making the higher the more attractive the player was. The second most important factors were batting average and home runs. These were each assigned a weight of 20%, and so on. The final stage is to multiple the ranks and the weights to find the winner.

Table 8.3

| | Batting Average | Home Runs | Runs Batted In | Salary (in mil) | Intangibles | Total |
|---|---|---|---|---|---|---|
| | | | **SMART Table** | | | |
| Weights | 20% | 20% | 10% | 40% | 10% | 100% |
| Player A | 0.8 | 2 | 0.8 | 1.6 | 0.7 | 5.9 |
| Player B | 1.2 | 1.6 | 0.9 | 2.4 | 0.8 | 6.9 |
| Player C | 1.6 | 1.2 | 1 | 3.2 | 0.9 | 7.9 |
| Player D | 2 | 0.8 | 0.7 | 4 | 1 | 8.5 |

The application of the SMART method results in Player D being selected. Based on the decision rule selected, Player D is the best mix of salary, performance and intangible skills. He will receive a contract offer. If he rejects it, the team will move on to Player C, or seek other players to sign.

Another method of performing the SMART analysis is simply by assigning points to the various factors, as follows:

Table 8.4

| | Batting Average | Home Runs | Runs Batted In | Salary (in mil) | Intangibles | Total |
|---|---|---|---|---|---|---|
| | | | **SMART Table With Points** | | | |
| Points | 20 | 20 | 10 | 40 | 10 | 100 |
| Player A | 6 | 10 | 8 | 16 | 7 | 47 |
| Player B | 12 | 16 | 9 | 24 | 8 | 69 |
| Player C | 16 | 12 | 10 | 32 | 9 | 79 |
| Player D | 20 | 8 | 7 | 40 | 10 | 85 |

In this version of SMART, the attributes are once again given weights, and points are assigned to each of the players attributes. The result is the same as in the previous example. Many people find this application of SMART much more difficult to do because assigning the point value seems more subjective than the ranking and weighting done in the first method of calculating SMART.

A third method of deploying SMART is by developing a **value tree**. A value tree is a multi-attribute decision tool linking objectives with sub-objectives and finally to the attributes of a decision. This method is especially useful when the qualitative aspects of the decision constitute a much greater percentage the final decision rule than qualitative attributes.

The first two decision nodes are usually the value of the quantifiable and the qualitative aspects of the decision. These values are then derived and plotted on a graph. So, using a value tree to assist in the selection of an office copier, the first two nodes are cost and intangible attributes. The cost node can have sub attributes such as initial cost of the copier, the estimated cost of maintenance and cost of supplies. The intangible attributes node can have such sub attributes as two-sided copying, color copying, collating and stapling.

**Figure 8.1**

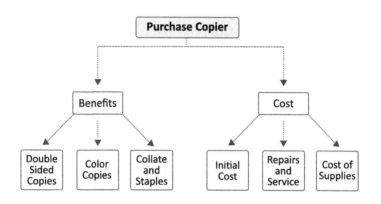

The value assigned to the cost and to the intangible assets can be used to develop an objective function that can be plotted on two axes. For sake of discussion, the three copier benefits will be measured in "utils". The decision-maker is evaluating seven copiers. Plotting the two attributes–cost and benefits–will result in a graph of an **efficient frontier**. Intuitively, the graph allows us to trade benefits against cost in the decision making process. Any option on the efficient frontier is said to **dominate** other options in the analysis. An example of the efficient frontier will be presented in the next chapter.

**Swing weights**[52] may also be employed when many qualitative attributes are being analyzed. Swing weights are a measure of utility that place a relative importance on the change between the worst ranking and the best ranking of one attribute versus the change in another. Swing weights are usually placed on an absolute scale with the highest value of say, 100, assigned to

---

52. It is a somewhat ironic title in a decision analysis book where there are many sports examples. The phrase swing weight is also used in describing golf clubs and baseball bats.

the best of the most important qualitative attribute. The worst possible score for this variable is set at 0. The range of the second most important qualitative variable is then set relative to the first variable. Suppose in our baseball player example we wished to expand the number of decision attributes by including speed and arm strength in the players' evaluations. Speed could be judged as the most important qualitative value and given a swing weight range of zero to 100. Arm strength, the second most important qualitative variable would then be ranked on a range of zero to 70. This type of weighting would continue until all qualitative attributes are considered and SMART is then utilized.

In this case the fictitious auditor of the most storied Major League Baseball team[53] used the SMART and swing weights to schedule audits based on risk to the organization.

The SMART method is fairly intuitive, but it does require two sets of somewhat subjective decisions: the ranking of attributes and the weights. These can cause controversy where there are multiple decision-makers as all may not agree on every weight or rank. This process becomes even more difficult when swing weights are introduced into the discussion.

---

53. Major League Baseball is a huge industry. While information about baseball ownership is not a matter of public record, it has been estimated the New York Yankee franchise is worth an estimated $5 billion. Risk assessment is not a trivial issue when dealing with such an organization. The cash flow and the marketing impact of a potential fraud would have major repercussions for not only the owners but the fans.

There is another potential problem with the SMART method. In the following example, four additional players have the following statistics:

**Table 8.5**

|  | Raw Statistics | | | | |
|---|---|---|---|---|---|
|  | Batting Average | Home Runs | Runs Batted In | Salary (in mil) | Total |
| Weights | 30% | 10% | 20% | 40% | 100% |
| Player E | 0.252 | **50** | 80 | 25 | |
| Player F | 0.283 | 45 | 95 | 12 | |
| Player G | 0.294 | 30 | **100** | 20 | |
| Player H | **0.311** | 20 | 70 | **10** | |

This time, the leaders in every category are demonstrated by a heavy border. The ranking for each attribute for each player is as follows:

**Table 8.6**

|  | Ranks and Weights | | | | |
|---|---|---|---|---|---|
|  | Batting Average | Home Runs | Runs Batted In | Salary (in mil) | Total |
| Weights | 30% | 10% | 20% | 40% | 100% |
| Player E | 4 | **10** | 6 | 2.5 | |
| Player F | 7 | 9 | 9 | 9 | |
| Player G | 8 | 6 | **10** | 5 | |
| Player H | **10** | 4 | 4 | **10** | |

The ranking once again follows the principle of the most desirable score receiving a ten, and other rankings being done relative to the highest score. The SMART Table is:

**Table 8.7**

<table>
<tr><td colspan="6" align="center">SMART Table</td></tr>
<tr><td></td><td>Batting Average</td><td>Home Runs</td><td>Runs Batted In</td><td>Salary (in mil)</td><td>Total</td></tr>
<tr><td>Weights</td><td>30%</td><td>10%</td><td>20%</td><td>40%</td><td>100%</td></tr>
<tr><td>Player E</td><td>1.2</td><td>1</td><td>1.2</td><td>1</td><td>4.4</td></tr>
<tr><td>Player F</td><td>2.1</td><td>0.9</td><td>1.8</td><td>3.6</td><td>8.4</td></tr>
<tr><td>Player G</td><td>2.4</td><td>0.6</td><td>2</td><td>2</td><td>7</td></tr>
<tr><td>Player H</td><td>3</td><td>0.4</td><td>0.8</td><td>4</td><td>8.2</td></tr>
</table>

Player F edges out Player H as the player selected. Interestingly enough, Player F was not the leader in any particular category, but his combination of skills and low salary was enough to make him the overall winner. Many regard this possibility as a potential weakness of the SMART method.

# Chapter Summary

◆ A particularly difficult type of decision to make is one with both qualitative and quantitative factors.

◆ The Simple Multi-Attribute Rating Technique (SMART) is one method of accomplishing this.

◆ SMART uses the importance of each factor (weights) and the relative ranking of each potential choice within a decision factor to arrive at a solution.

◆ Drawing a value tree first can help insure all the relevant decision attributes are captured.

◆ SMART depends on some subjective judgements to arrive at a decision. This could be a difficulty if multiple decision- makers are involved.

◆ Doing a SMART table can be a lot of work as the decision- maker needs to define the ranks and weights. In the next chapter, other potentially easier methodologies will be examined.

# Discussion Questions

1. Using the SMART methodology, analyze four potential vacation spots with four different decision factors: Cost, scenery, gambling locations, and tourist sights.

   Hint: The gambling location may be treated as either a binary decision (yes or no, or 0 and 1) or it may be ranked as any other quantitative factor. Begin your analysis by drawing the value tree.

2. You have been offered two jobs, with the third option remaining where you are. A fourth option is attempting to negotiate an increase in salary at your current job. Perform a SMART analysis on this situation.

   Hint: How do you factor risk into this decision? Afterall, your employer may simply fire you if you reveal you have been speaking with other potential employers!

3. **Using the year 2000 as a base year, how successful were the Oakland Athletics in implementing their strategy?**

**Hint:** Your answer should encompass data for 20 years and be expressed as a cost-benefit analysis. For example, a Major League baseball team plays 162 game per year. There is a winner or loser in every game. Therefore, the average number of victories for every team across the league is 82 games. One meaningful way to express the data is: The average player payroll for the Oakland Athletics has been x% of the average Major League baseball team salary, but they have won "y" number of games per year. After completing the analysis, evaluate the decision to use "Moneyball" tactics.

---

*Solutions to the above questions can be downloaded from*
*the* **Online Resources** *section of this book on*
**www.vibrantpublishers.com**

---

# Chapter 9

# EBA and Even Swaps

SMART is not the only way to balance qualitative and quantitative factors. The Elimination by Aspects (EBA) and Even Swaps methodologies can be used too. This chapter reviews some of the intricacies of these methods as an alternative to SMART.

As we have seen, the application of SMART requires two sets of potentially subjective judgments. While the process itself is relatively easy to use, the amount of time and energy put into the SMART analysis can be fairly large. It is easy to see how a SMART analysis can bog down if several decision-makers are involved, each of whom have their own rankings and weights.

Amos Tversky proposed another alternative, called the **elimination by aspects** (EBA) method. EBA is a **non-compensatory** rather than a **compensatory method** such as SMART. As you may recall from a previous chapter, the SMART method could produce a "winner" in a multi-attribute decision even though the "winner" did not rank first in any particular decision attribute. This not possible with EBA since the decision-maker must list and rank each decision attribute by importance.

"Cutoffs" are established for the most important factor. All choices that do not meet the cut-off are eliminated from further consideration. A cutoff is established for the second most important factor and alternatives not meeting the second cutoff are then eliminated. The process continues with the evaluation of attributes until a clear winner emerges.

Let's return to our baseball team example again to see how EBA works.

**Table 9.1**

| | Raw Statistics | | | | |
|---|---|---|---|---|---|
| | Batting Average | Home Runs | Runs Batted In | Salary (in mil) | Intangibles |
| **Player A** | 0.251 | 50 | 80 | 25 | 7 |
| **Player B** | 0.272 | 40 | 90 | 20 | 8 |
| **Player C** | 0.293 | 30 | 100 | 15 | 9 |
| **Player D** | 0.313 | 20 | 70 | 10 | 10 |

We choose the most important decision factor. In our SMART methodology we weighted salary as the most important factor since the team had a limited budget. After a careful analysis, it appears the team can't afford to pay an individual player more than $20 million. Despite having impressive on field playing statistics, Player A is eliminated, and the team moves on to the next attribute and consideration of the remaining players. Homeruns and batting average were deemed to be equally important. The team chooses to break the tie with a qualitative decision. Followers of sabermetrics generally believe batting average is better indicator of skill than home runs. They decide a batting average of at least .280 is desirable for the amount of money the player will eventually command, eliminating Player B from further consideration. The team then moves onto the third attribute, home runs. They believe the player has to hit more than ten home runs in a season in order to draw fans into the stadium. Fans love homeruns so a player hitting less than ten home runs would draw negative reactions from the fans. After putting all of this together, we find Player C is choice. The fourth and fifth criteria, runs batted in, and intangibles do not even enter into the calculation.

**Table 9.2**

| Elimination by Aspects Table | | | |
|---|---|---|---|
| **Rank** | **Aspect** | **Cutoff** | **Result** |
| 1 | Salary | < 20 | Player A Eliminated |
| 2 | BA | > .279 | Player B Eliminated |
| 3 | HR | > 10 | Player D Eliminated |
| **Winner** | | | **Player C Selected** |

In this particular case, the decision to look at batting average ahead of homeruns did not have an adverse impact on the decision. It is possible the order the attributes are evaluated could conceivably result in a different decision. More on that later.

# 9.1 Even Swaps

Another decision making methodology is the **even swaps** method. This process focuses on coming to a decision through the use of trade-offs or swapping one attribute for another. Before we begin a further description of even swaps, it is necessary to define some terms. One option is said to **dominate** another option if all attributes of that option are better than the attributes of a second option.

We can illustrate that by using an example from financial theory. The expected return from an investment portfolio is driven by the amount of risk in the portfolio. The universe of potential portfolios is shown on the graph as points exhibiting different combinations of risk (measured by standard deviation of the returns) and the expected return. The upper portion of the **efficient frontier** contains the portfolios dominating other portfolios. A simple exercise will demonstrate this. If you move upward on any point from the x axis to a point under the upper portion of the efficient frontier, you can always get a higher return for the same amount of risk by moving to the point on the efficient frontier. There is no portfolio of investments that can exceed this amount of return. Therefore, any point on the efficient frontier is said to dominate any other point below it. You can repeat the exercise by moving to the right from the y axis. If you move past the upper portion of the efficient frontier you will once again find you can limit your risk and achieve the same return by adopting the portfolio moving you back onto the efficient frontier.[54]

---

54. The optimal portfolio is the portfolio tangent to the efficient frontier. Many of you will recognize this as the derivative. More on constrained optimization later.

**Figure 9.1**

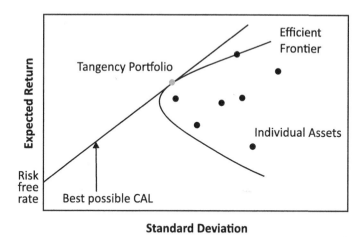

Similarly, a **practically dominated option** is one where the values for the vast majority of that options' attributes are exceeded by those of another option. The superiority or equality of the value of remaining attributes of the practically dominated option are deemed to be too small or inconsequential to overcome the superiority of the first option's attributes. Using practical domination means the even swaps method is a compensatory strategy, allowing the lack or deficiency of one or more attributes to be compensated for by its superiority in other attributes.

Even swaps proceed in the following manner. First, reduce the complexity of the decision matrix by eliminating as many dominated or practically dominated options are possible. Then eliminate an attribute by performing even swaps. Continue this process until a winner is selected. Let's use our baseball example to illustrate the even swaps method.

We start with our raw statistics and the same problem. We can only sign one player to a contract.

**Table 9.3**

| | Raw Statistics | | | | |
|---|---|---|---|---|---|
| | Batting Average | Home Runs | Runs Batted In | Salary (in mil) | Intangibles |
| **Player A** | 0.251 | 50 | 80 | 25 | 7 |
| **Player B** | 0.272 | 40 | 90 | 20 | 8 |
| **Player C** | 0.293 | 30 | 100 | 15 | 9 |
| **Player D** | 0.313 | 20 | 70 | 10 | 10 |

The first step is to reduce the size of the decision matrix by removing all dominated or practically dominated options. For the sake of this presentation, let's assume the team has determined it can't afford more than $20 million per year for this player, no matter how much his statistics warrant it. This is a form of practical domination, so Player A is removed from consideration.

The even swaps process then begins. Intangibles is the first attribute to be examined. As you recall, the players' intangible assets such as leadership and work ethic were rated on a scale of 1 to 10, with the leader for that attribute being assigned a ten and the other players judged with that as the reference point. The team reckons a one-point change in the value of the intangible traits of the athlete is equivalent to about two homeruns per year.

**Table 9.4**

| | Even Swap on Intangible Assets | | | | |
|---|---|---|---|---|---|
| | Batting Average | Home Runs | Runs Batted In | Salary (in mil) | Intangibles |
| Player B | 0.272 | 36 | 90 | 20 | 10 |
| Player C | 0.293 | 28 | 100 | 15 | 10 |
| Player D | 0.313 | 20 | 70 | 10 | 10 |

According to this calculus, if Player B had higher intangible assets (a rating of 10), He would only need to hit 36 home runs, a decrease of four from the original decision matrix. The same reasoning applies to Player C. If he had an intangible rating of 10, he would need to hit two less homeruns. This process did not eliminate any Players from consideration, but it did eliminate one attribute.

The even swap process continues by evaluating homeruns. The team judges someone hitting 20 homeruns in a year should earn approximately $10 million dollars per year, the amount Player D is being paid.

**Table 9.5**

| | Even Swap on Home Runs | | | |
|---|---|---|---|---|
| | Batting Average | Home Runs | Runs Batted In | Salary (in mil) |
| Player B | 0.272 | 20 | 90 | 10 |
| Player C | 0.293 | 20 | 100 | 10 |
| Player D | 0.313 | 20 | 70 | 10 |

This now allows the home runs and salary attributes to be removed from future consideration. After this even swap, Player C now clearly dominates Player B, who can be removed from the decision matrix.

Another iteration is needed so RBIs will now be considered in terms of batting average. The team simply calculates a ratio of the two players' RBIs and applies it to the batting averages.

Table 9.6

| Final Decision Table | | |
|---|---|---|
| | Batting Average | Runs Batted In |
| Player C | 0.332 | 70 |
| Player D | 0.313 | 70 |

Player D is eliminated because his statistics were dominated by Player C. The advantage in RBIs was simply too great to be compensated for by Player D's superior batting average.

There are some criticisms of the Even Swaps method. First, this can be very hard to do unless you have a lot of practice. Secondly, it is possible the very process could have an impact on the outcome. A decision-maker may be inconsistent when performing the swaps or continue to take into account attributes that have been eliminated. Afterall, it may be difficult for a decision-maker to remove the most important attribute from consideration. Determining what alternatives are subject to practical dominance can also be a difficult decision.

## 9.2 Other Alternatives to SMART

There are two other alternatives to SMART worth mentioning for the sake of completeness, but they will not be considered in this book.

The first is the **Simple Multiple Attribute Rating Technique Exploiting Ranks, or SMARTER**. This is a simplified version of SMART that assumes attribute values are linear. It also does not require the relative ranking of attributes (i.e. the best choice within an attribute is rated as a 10 and the other options are rated in relation to that) but simply ranks them ordinally (first, second, third, etc.)

The **analytical hierarchy process (AHP)** was developed by **Thomas Saaty**. It entails setting up a decision hierarchy and then making pairwise comparisons of attributes and alternatives. The comparisons are turned into weights, leading to a provisional decision. This can be a complex process often requiring a large number of comparisons. There are several software packages available to apply AHP, including EXPERT CHOICE, developed by Saaty.

## 9.3 Will You Always Get the Same Result?

As we have just seen different decision methodologies could result in different choices. In this somewhat contrived exercise, the EBA, SMART and Even Swaps methodologies produced a different winner.

Sometimes even the order we process the data in can influence the decision. **Satisficing** was a term originated by Herbert Simon, winner of the Nobel Prize in Economics. Simon's research focused on the cognitive limitations and time constraints of decision-makers. We can all intuitively understand this perspective. Our decision making process is sometimes overloaded by too many choices to evaluate correctly and too little time to do that. We often run out of time before we can absorb all of the information, we need to make the "best decision". Simon believed a decision-maker will review alternatives until a minimally acceptable choice appears. That minimally acceptable alternative will most likely be adopted by the decision-maker who will move on to the next challenge.

There is no question about the validity of Simon's theory as we do this all the time. Satisficing is an efficient use of time and energy when the return and the risk are both low, but it does have its limitations. For instance, it can be very annoying to a customer. Imagine yourself in line at the Division of Motor Vehicles. You have a unique problem with your driver's license. There is no incentive for the attendant to take any risk at all in making a decision. The first, least risky alternative will be chosen, especially since the attendant wants to move through as many cases as possible. It will almost be certainly "kicked-up" to the supervisor. It might take some time for you to find someone who will make the necessary decision!

Let's look at a busy regional bank manager responsible for a dozen banking locations. She must staff many positions at these locations, and time is of the essence. In such a situation, the regional manager may satisfice, and choose the first candidates she encounters meeting the minimum requirements. An advertised job search may have hundreds of applicants. There also may be multiple openings. The manager may make a decision based on certain attributes and the amount of time available to make the decision. Clearly, this is rational behavior, but it does not guarantee the regional manager will hire the best candidates only acceptable candidates.

Let's look at our baseball team and an example of **satisficing**. Assume the decision-maker has the same three criteria used in the EBA example. If he reviews the players by jointly considering all three success criteria, then Player C will again by chosen. However, if the decision-maker applies the decision rules sequentially, with salary being the first attribute processed then Player B could be selected since he is right at the salary cut-off and will be the second person evaluated. Satisficing is heavily dependent not only on the order data is processed but whether all success criteria are applied. To achieve the same result as EBA multiple passes must be made through the data, more time-consuming than satisficing. In our baseball example, SMART, EBA, and satisficing may come up with three different answers, all rational in their own context. This realization is in stark contrast to the economic man, who with perfect information will make the correct economic decision every time.

A few words on satisficing. All economic models make assumptions about reality. I have never personally seen managers make all of their decisions by satisficing. As anecdotal as it is, my experience has shown most managers will attempt to process all available information and then make the best decision based on the information available at that time. Satisficing can occur as time runs out for the decision. A famous chess player observing a game said one of the players was making only adequate moves in a position and not the best moves, so he had no hope of gaining an advantage. The same happens in the business world as well. Too many adequate decisions instead of the best decisions can result in a company having trouble competing in the marketplace.

# Chapter Summary

◆ The Economic Man possesses perfect information, perfect processing capability, and sufficient time to assess choices and make the best decision. Behavioral economics and behavioral finance have attacked these assumptions.

◆ Multi-attribute decisions can be the most difficult to make since they often require an analysis of qualitative and quantitative data.

◆ The Simple Multi-Attribute Rating Technique (SMART) applies a system of ranking and weights to make decisions when the decision criteria have disparate characteristics.

◆ The Elimination by Aspects system makes a decision by selecting the most important attribute and applying a decision rule ("cutoff") to that attribute. If there are several possible alternatives remaining the decision-maker applies the same process to the next most important attribute. This process is continued until a decision is made.

◆ The Even Swaps method trades "amounts" of attributes with each other until a dominant solution is reached.

◆ There is often no one right decision. The option finally chosen by the decision-maker is heavily dependent on the methodology selected and sometimes the order the data is processed in.

## Discussion Questions

1. Go back to the previous chapter. Using the even swaps and EBA process, review your selection of vacation spots. Did your answer change?

2. Do you satisfice when you make decisions? If so, under what conditions do you satisfice?

---

*Solutions to the above questions can be downloaded from* *the* **Online Resources** *section of this book on* **www.vibrantpublishers.com**

# Chapter **10**

# Sensitivity Analysis

A fter we complete our decision-analysis and come to a conclusion, are we finished with the process? Definitely not. Sensitivity analysis checks what happens to our decision if some of the underlying data or assumptions change. This chapter demonstrates two of the most common ways to perform sensitivity analysis.

Any decision entails judgment. Sometimes those judgments turn out to be incorrect. Any judgment, and therefore any decision is subject to risks and uncertainties. This is particularly true when trying to forecast the future. Take the typical budgeting process. Sales managers and department heads are asked to give their best estimate of what will happen in the next year. They may provide a one-point estimate for each of the revenue and expense items they are responsible for. Sometimes these will be low estimates, particularly if they will be held accountable for and receive compensation based on achieving their forecasts.[55]

---

55. Often referred to as "sandbagging the forecast."

Even with the best intentions and best efforts of those responsible, the budget will be subject to risk. How can senior managers reduce the risk and uncertainty? One way is through sensitivity analysis. This is a structured review of the assumptions and possible outcomes for all of variables in the model. There are various ways to perform sensitivity analysis so only one will be demonstrated here.

Let's set up a hypothetical budget preparation. You are the Chief Financial Officer of a public company. You need to provide budget information to the board of directors and operating management for the upcoming year. The SEC also encourages you to provide forward looking information in your filings with the Commission for the benefit of the investing public. Consequently, the company needs a robust budgeting system.

Your management team provides the following information for a new product:

- Sales forecast of $1,250,000. This is the most likely number. The optimistic estimate is $2,000,000. The low, or pessimistic number is $1,000,000

- The operations department estimates the cost of goods sold will be 75% of the sales volume.

- The fixed overhead will be $100,000 to $200,000.

How should the CFO proceed?

# 10.1 Kicking the Tires

Budgeting always begins with the underlying revenue assumptions. The first step is to see how robust are. The sales manager will be asked some tough questions to ascertain how reasonable his sales forecast is. Some are these questions are:

- What customers will buy the new products? What percentage of the forecasted sales will go to current customers? It is much easier to sell to current customers rather than finding new customers.

- Will the company need to find new customers for this product to meet its budget? How realistic is it to assume sales to new customers? We know from the endowment effect competitors will fight fiercely to save their customers.

- At what price should the product be sold? What marketing support will it need?

- As sales moves towards the high end of the range or the low end of the range, will the company be able to keep its margins? Increasing sales sometimes requires prices be dropped. Conversely, to prevent deteriorating sales a price cut, or marketing campaign may be required.

After answering all of the questions, the sales manager provides the probable range of sales as being a low of $1,000,000 and a high of $2,000,000, with the most likely scenario still being $1,250,000. When pressed, he is extremely confident of the high and low points of the range, as well as the most likely forecasted sales of $1,250,000.

The operations manager will be required to defend the estimate of the cost of goods sold with questions such as:

- How confident are you with the labor, material and overhead costs you will have to incur?

- Will vendors keep the same pricing if the sales volume declines or increases?

- Can you secure enough labor at the required wage rate to manufacture the product?

- Does the company have the required capacity to manufacture all the other products as well as this new product?

- Will the company need to work weekends and overtime to manufacture this product?

- How much will the marginal cost of production rise with an increase in volume?

The operations manager is extremely confident about manufacturing the product at the budgeted rates. The labor will be provided by a union at the contracted for labor rates. The price and supply of raw material has been previously protected with forward commitment contracts and other hedges. The plant has excess capacity so the allocation of overhead and the plant capacity will not be an issue.

Finally, the marketing manager will be asked what advertising support the product will need to for sales at the proposed level. She thought there was a possibility the company would need up to $100,000 in new marketing and volume discounts to achieve the high range of the sales spectrum, but as of right now she did not know. This company could be forced to expend that much to entice major retailers to sell the new product. This amount was added to the $100,000 manufacturing fixed cost the operations manager had projected, resulting in a fixed cost range of $100,000 to $200,000. Since one point is no better estimate than the other in the range, the midpoint of $150,000 will be used in the sensitivity analysis.

## 10.2 High-Low Sensitivity Analysis

The first step is to use the high-low method of analyzing the forecast. This simply takes all three estimates and puts them in a tabular format, as follows:

**Table 10.1**

|  | Low–Pessimistic | Most Likely | High–Optimistic |
|---|---|---|---|
| Sales | $1,000,000 | $1,250,000 | $2,000,000 |
| Cost of Sales | 750,000 | 937,500 | 1,500,000 |
| Fixed Costs | 100,000 | 150,000 | 200,000 |
| Net Profit | $150,000 | $162,500 | $300,000 |

This provides a preliminary analysis of the situation and it looks like the product will actually be modestly profitable in the first year. Is this the end of the analysis? In this case no. The CFO then uses a financial heuristic breakeven, to make a quick risk approximation. In this situation, breakeven sales are $600,000, or $150,000 divided by 25% (the gross profit on each unit of sales). He believes this is an extremely likely event given the forecast and therefore moves on to the next level of analysis, a Monte Carlo simulation.

The Monte Carlo simulation checks the risk of a forecast. It builds a model of predicted results by randomly substituting a range of values for each variable. A large number of scenarios will be run, each time using randomly generated results for each variable. There are many commercially available software packages such as Desdi (Apple Product) or Argo (Booz Allen) to run Monte Carlo simulations.[56] The following is the result table for 1,000 trails generated by Desdi:

**Table 10.2**

| | Variable Type | Distribution | Low Value | Average Result | High Value |
|---|---|---|---|---|---|
| **Sales** | Range | Triangular | $1,012,172 | $1,416,319 | $1,967,194 |
| **COGS** | Formula | Calculation | 759,129 | 1,062,239 | 1,475,396 |
| **Overhead** | Range | Triangular | 100,795 | 151,159 | 198,072 |

More trials can be run, but it is easy to see from the first 1,000 trials the product will again be marginally profitable at best.

Suppose the CFO wishes to change the parameters of the experiment. Perhaps the sales manager is relatively new to the job, and the CFO has some doubts as to the most likely sales number. Instead of using a triangular distribution (one with a range and a most likely estimate), the simulation is now run with sales being calculated as a normal distribution (bell shaped curve).

---

56. Both packages are free to download.

The results table now looks like:

**Table 10.3**

| | Variable Type | Distribution | Low Value | Average Result | High Value |
|---|---|---|---|---|---|
| **Sales** | Range | Normal-90% | $590,431 | $1,499,538 | $2,434,237 |
| **COGS** | Formula | Calculation | 442,823 | $1,124,654 | 1,825,678 |
| **Overhead** | Range | Normal-90% | 63,040 | 150,425 | 245,237 |

The judgment about the product is still the same. It will most likely be marginally profitable. The Monte Carlo simulation and the break-even analysis gives the decision-maker confidence the risk is relatively low for this product as will the profits. Since there is available manufacturing capacity and a qualitative reason to manufacture the product (keeping competitors away from the customer base), the CFO allows the project to proceed.[57]

---

57. The data visualization of a Monte Carlo simulation can be done through a **tornado chart** (easily constructed on Excel).

# Chapter Summary

◆ Decisions need to be tested before they are implemented. Decisions often rely on assumptions and forecasts. There is always risk and uncertainty in any assumption.

◆ The first step in a sensitivity analysis is to test the assumptions of the data through critical reasoning and questioning. The assumptions must be grounded in reality and as bias free as possible.

◆ Financial heuristics then can be used to quickly examine the data. These include the use of the high-low sensitivity, payback period, and breakeven point analysis.

◆ If it seems the decision is still acceptable both in terms of risk and reward, a high-low estimate can be made. Finally, a Monte Carlo simulation can be run to more thoroughly test the assumptions.

## Discussion Questions

1. Using the same example in this chapter, increase the low, most likely, and high estimate of the fixed costs by $100,000. Compute the new breakeven analysis and the high-low sensitivity analysis. Does this change the decision?

2. Download one of the free Monte Carlo simulation software available on the internet. Change the parameters of the example in this chapter as follows:

   a. Change the distribution of sales to a uniform distribution.

   b. Increase the low, most likely and high estimate of the fixed costs by $100,000

   Do these changes impact the decision? If so, why?

> *Solutions to the above questions can be downloaded from*
> *the* **Online Resources** *section of this book on*
> **www.vibrantpublishers.com**

*This page is intentionally left blank*

# Chapter **11**

# Negotiating and Selling the Final Decision

A fter we complete our decision analysis and come to a conclusion, we may have to negotiate the details of that decision with other stakeholders in the decision. This chapter provides some pointers on good negotiating practices as well as some negotiating strategies suggested by game theory.

## 11.1 Negotiations

Sometimes decisions depend on negotiations with a third party or approval by internal stakeholders. Negotiations are a common feature of life. We do it all the time. Think about making any major purchase, such as a house or a car. There is usually a lot of back and forth between the buyer and seller in such situations. Salary negotiations are also common when we change jobs. In a very real sense, negotiating is an example of a **strategic interaction**, where two or more people or organizations compete against each other.

Some basic rules of negotiations are:

1. **All parties need to profit from a deal, or at least be left at the status quo**. This is probably the most important rule of negotiations. We have heard stories of unscrupulous negotiators taking advantage of other parties, but these apocalyptic negotiations take place only when one of the parties is desperate to complete deal. The wisdom of doing this is suspect. Taking advantage of those you regularly deal with will often not work out well in the long run.

2. **The party who needs the deal least is able to do the best at the negotiating table**. One party to the negotiations will be able to extract concessions from the parties who need to complete the deal. This can happen for various reasons such as access to critical resources or sometimes just for prestige.

3. **Be prepared before the negotiation begins**. It is extremely beneficial to understand and anticipate what the positions and objections of other parties will be. Well run organizations will give instructions to their negotiators about what is acceptable and what is not. They will also have controls on the negotiators. We are all familiar when someone attempts to secure a loan from a bank. If it is a sufficient size, the loan officer will need to have a supervisor, or a senior management committee approve the loan. No deal is final until the committee puts their stamp of approval on it. The supervisor or the committee serves as a brake on bad decisions by the loan officer and provides negotiating input to him.

4. **Do not become emotionally tied to the negotiation**. It has been said cool heads prevail. That is nowhere more evident than at the negotiating table.

5. **Try not to negotiate alone.** Sometimes this can't be avoided, but it is always good to have someone accompany you when negotiating. They can prevent you from making costly errors in the negotiation and are witnesses to the discussion. It is sometimes easy to overlook the obvious or not be quick enough on our feet to understand all of the nuances in the negotiation or the implications of a proposal.

6. **Careful preparation is required for summit meetings.** Negotiations done by the head of an organization can seal a deal and save time. Unfortunately, this can be extremely risky since there may be no appeal from a bad negotiating situation. The head of an organization should only be brought into the negotiation when all substantive matters have been resolved. A corollary of this is no negotiating should be allowed when the final agreements are going to be signed.

7. **Negotiations have a life of their own.** Taking too long to negotiate can jeopardize the proposed deal. Negotiations taking too long to get done often suffer from "deal fatigue". Parties come to believe they are being "nickel and dimed" and run out of patience.

8. **Negotiate globally.** Issues can be dealt with sequentially, but final acceptance of any one negotiating point should be deferred until all issues are resolved. This is the principle of **linkage**, made famous by Henry Kissinger. Individual positions can be traded for a final global solution. Notwithstanding this advice, it is important to remember the endowment effect. Once a party believes something has been settled in its favor, trying to take it back can be difficult. Parties will not give something up lightly in a negotiation. For instance, negotiators with unions

understand the previous labor contract will be starting point for the new negotiation. The union will fight to retain something it has already "won" in a previous negotiation. Multiple issue negotiations should always be punctuated with reminders a tentative agreement on one point is subject to achieving a global agreement.

## 11.2 Asymmetric Information

One major problem with negotiating is each party can have **asymmetric information**. This is a situation where each of the participants do not have the same information. One or more parties to the negotiation has superior information, giving them an advantage in the negotiations. This is a particularly acute problem when the negotiation is seen as a "one-time" interaction. The parties having the "knowledge" advantage may have an incentive to misrepresent it to the parties who don't. Alternatively, they may reveal only a portion of the truth, and not the entire truth during the negotiation.

How can an asymmetric information advantage be overcome? There are several ways:

1. Investing resources to find information. A simple example of this is using the internet to conduct research on the opposing party's positions.

2. Using third party experts such as consultants, auditors and rating agencies.

3. Insisting on contractual representations and warranties. This is a standard procedure when negotiating a major contract.

In certain situations, the side with the superior knowledge may signal their intention. This is done to prove the validity of the claims by the party with the superior knowledge. A common example of signaling in a negotiation is to put up collateral for your position. A borrower signals their intent to pay back a loan by pledging something of value to the lender for payment of the loan. Not only does the value of the collateral provide a cushion to the lender, but it also brings the endowment effect into play, particularly if the borrower has sentimental or emotional attachment to the collateral. The borrower will make sure to pay back the loan to avoid the feeling of loss associated with any collateral.

Reputation is also an important factor in dealing with a party having superior knowledge, particularly if the transactions are repetitive. A reputation is the public perception about a person, organization or product built up over time. For instance, a company having a "roll-up" strategy in their industry (i.e. acquiring other smaller companies to eliminate competition and create economies of scale) may acquire a reputation for negotiating honestly and treating the employees of the acquired companies fairly after the mergers. A company in an acquisition mode knows word will spread quickly if it breaks promises made during negotiations. Doing this a number of times will result in no one willing to sell to them. Reputations are a major asset when negotiating. However, a good reputation can be destroyed quickly with just a few thoughtless actions.

## 11.3 Coordination Problems

Coming away with no deal is sometimes worse than a minimally satisfactory deal. Consider the case of a contentious divorce, where continued litigation eats up the financial resources of both parties. Both sides lose if no agreement is reached. It soon becomes apparent no deal may in fact be worse than a bad deal as life savings are dissipated in litigation. This is known as the coordination problem of negotiating. Even if there is asymmetric information, the party having this advantage could share information or signal to the other party to try and bring negotiations to an end before financial catastrophe results.

## 11.4 Game Theory

Game theory has been used in such diverse fields as politics, business strategy and war gaming. An early antecedent of game theory was Pascal's Wager. The famous mathematician Blaise Pascal (1623-1662) proposed the following argument for why it was good to believe in God's existence:

**Table 11.1**

|                  | God Exists          | God Doesn't Exist |
|------------------|---------------------|-------------------|
| **You Believe**  | Eternal Bliss       | No Downside       |
| **You Don't Believe** | Eternal Punishment | No Downside       |

Pascal was attempting to show belief in God was completely logical. There Is nothing but upside![58]

A more modern demonstration of game theory is the Prisoner's Dilemma. Two suspects are apprehended at the scene of the crime. They are interrogated separately. The prosecutor offers each of them a plea bargain, as follows:

**Table 11.2**

|  | B Stays Silent | B Betrays A |
|---|---|---|
| **A Stays Silent** | (-1,-1) | (-5,0) |
| **A Betrays B** | (0,-5) | (-2,-2) |

Suspect A will walk away with no jail time if he betrays Suspect B, who will receive a five-year sentence. Prisoner B is offered the same deal if he betrays Suspect A. The best decision is for both to remain silent. The total jail time will be two years. However, there is no incentive for either to remain silent because they are each threatened with a five-year jail sentence. The suspects will probably reach an equilibrium point and betray each other, receiving a total of four years in prison. This is not a **Pareto efficient** solution, as both players would be better off if they coordinated their answers and trusted each other.[59]

---

58. There are many counters to this argument. It is presented here only for the purpose of context.

59. A Pareto efficient solution is one where no one person can be made better off without making someone else (another player) worse off.

Some of the most important characteristics of game theory are demonstrated by the Prisoner's Dilemma:

1. The payoff table is crucial to the final decision of each **player**.

2. An equilibrium point may not be the optimal point from the perspective of both players.

3. Charitable instincts will often result in a loss to one of the players. A or B could have stayed silent, and allowed their confederate to go free, but at a personal cost.

4. Anticipating the reaction of the other players is a critical part of the game.

Game theory provides some strategies that are useful in negotiating and decision making:

1. **Maximax**–This is the strategy of a risk taker. The strategy yielding the highest potential return is chosen, no matter what the risk. A gambler has a maximax mindset. People facing several options each of which will result in a sure loss will often become risk-takers.

2. **Minimax**– A strategy minimizing the maximum loss a player can sustain. Insurance companies settling lawsuits employ a minimax strategy. Rather than risking a trial, they negotiate settlements to contain their losses.

3. **Maximin**– A strategy maximizing the minimum return for a player. Stockbrokers locking into gains by selling stock at a predetermined price employ a maximin strategy.

4. **Mixed**–Picking a random strategy. The player will pick a random move from a set of possibilities. The goal is to become unpredictable. This works well when a party

discovers a pattern in the other player's strategy. A simple example is the popular children's game of "Rocks, Papers, Scissors". Someone falling into a pattern of calling "Scissors" every time can be defeated consistently by the other player calling "Rocks". The correct strategy is to randomly select one of the options every time.[60] The is to become unpredictable in order to win.

# 11.5 Walking Away From the Deal

Unfortunately, threats are sometimes made when negotiating. A threat conveys the meaning to the other parties one party is at their breaking point. Additional concessions are not possible and/or concessions from the other parties are needed to continue the negotiation. The party making the threat may have constituencies that must be satisfied or there may be minimum conditions the party has to satisfy to avoid personal consequences.

Common threats heard in negotiations are "take it or leave it" and "I will walk". An effective threat must be credible. Incredible threats often serve to weaken a negotiating position. The party making the threat must be ready to suffer the consequences if they are called on to carry it out. Sometimes the results can be devastating to all sides. Therefore, making threats should not be done out of emotion but from a detached, analytical perspective. One situation where the threat to walk away can work is when the other party makes an outrageous suggestion. Walking away and saying the negotiation needs to restart at a more reasonable

---

60. **John von Neumann (1903-1957)** did some of the original work on this strategy in the game of "Matching Pennies".

position can prevent the first unacceptable proposal from becoming the anchor in the discussion.

Threatening to walk away from a negotiation can be a bluff. Bluffing works best when the parties interact infrequently or only once. Of course, having the bluff called will often result in detrimental consequences to the bluffer.

## 11.6 Selling the Decision

After the decision analysis is completed and the decision is made and assessed, it may become necessary to convince other stakeholders in the organization it is correct. In common parlance, it will become necessary to "line-up" the decision-makers and make a presentation to gain their approval. While this is not a book about presentations, here are some hints about making an effective presentation:

- **Preparation is again key.** You must not only know your material; you must present both the advantages and disadvantages of the project.

- **Anticipate questions**. If you were the decision-maker, what would you be most concerned about?

- **Come prepared with a written presentation**. This presentation should include an executive summary of one page followed by a narrative description of the proposed decision and exhibits and charts.

- **Use graphics as much as possible.** It has been said a picture is worth a thousand words. A graph is worth five hundred. This is even more true in the era of Big Data, where visualization becomes even more important.

- **Don't force the audience to do analysis**. Think about how many times you have been presented with a chart and are then forced to analyze that chart. When presented with such a chart, the audience focuses on it and loses the speaker. A properly prepared chart will have a text box explaining what the information is meant to portray. The cognitive processing resources of the audience is limited. Try not to force them into using their System 2 as much as possible.

# Chapter Summary

◆ After a decision is made, it must sometimes be negotiated with other parties or "sold" to other stakeholders in the organization.

◆ The most important rule of negotiating is everyone must profit or at least left in the status quo from the decision or the transaction.

◆ Asymmetric information confers an advantage to one party in the negotiation. How and if it is used in the negotiation will depend on the circumstances of the negotiation.

◆ The coordination problem exists when having no deal is worse than even a minimally acceptable deal.

◆ Game theory provides several different strategy options a negotiator should understand and be familiar with. Needless to say, the negotiator must understand the organization's risk tolerance to understand which negotiating strategy to employ.

◆ Threats and bluffs are part of negotiating. A threat needs to be credible for it to be taken seriously. Bluffing generally works best when parties interact infrequently or only once.

# Discussion Questions

1. Do threats have a place in negotiations? If so, when and how should they be utilized?

2. Why are presentation skills and data visualization techniques exceptionally important when dealing with Big Data?

3. Describe the difference between a maximin and a minimax strategy. Provide an illustration of each.

4. The Prisoners' Dilemma seems like it is a simplistic example of game theory. Is it? Describe some other situations where the Prisoners' Dilemma applies.

5. When might you employ a mixed strategy?

*Solutions to the above questions can be downloaded from the* **Online Resources** *section of this book on* **www.vibrantpublishers.com**

*This page is intentionally left blank*

# Glossary

**A**ffect – The feeling of "good" or "bad" attached to a decision.

**All events test** – A test developed by the United States Internal Revenue Service virtually removing probability from deciding if tax deductions are valid. Under this test a valid deduction occurs when all events fixing the amount of the liability have occurred.

**All in cost** – The total cost incurred in any transaction, including explicit costs and opportunity costs.

**Anchoring and adjustment** – A heuristic suggesting decision-makers start at a reference point and make adjustments to the reference point based on additional events or information to reach their final decision.

**Asymmetrical dominance effect** – Another name for the decoy effect.

**Asymmetric information** – One party to a negotiation or a transaction has more material knowledge than the other parties.

**At the margin** – In economic theory, the intersection of marginal benefit and marginal cost. This is an equilibrium point and the optimal result.

**Attribute** – A factor to consider in decision making.

**Availability heuristic** – A heuristic for making decisions based on what comes to a decision-maker's mind. It depends heavily on the ability to recall examples. Something that comes to mind easily is deemed to be more probable.

**B**ayes Theorem – The probability of an event occurring based on prior knowledge of factors related to the event. The notation for Bayes Theorem is:

$$\frac{P(A \mid B) = P(B \mid A) \times P(A)}{P(B)}$$

**Behavioral economics** – The study of the impact non-economic effects such as bounded rationality has on decisions and how they are different than those predicted by classical economic theory.

**Behavioral finance** – A branch of behavioral economics studying the decision making of investors. It assumes investors are influenced by many factors and are not always or necessarily rational in their decision making.

**Bernoulli, Daniel (1700-1782)** – Pioneering Swiss statistician in the fields of probability and utility.

**Beta** – A measure of the investment risk of a portfolio compared to the market as defined. A beta of 2 indicates a 1% change in the market will cause a 2% change in the portfolio.

**Beyond a reasonable doubt** – A judicial standard of proof in a criminal trial. This requires a jury or judge be virtually certain of an event's occurrence before a decision can be reached.

**Bias** – Prejudice for or against particular options in a decision.

**Big Bath** – An attempt by a company to package and write-off all known problems in one announcement.

**Big Decision** – A decision requiring organized thinking and often requiring explanations to another party.

**Black Swan Event** – A totally unexpected event with a very low probability of occurrence that has major consequences.

**Blink** – A book by Malcolm Gladwell describing how humans can seemingly make decisions without thinking.[61]

**Brainstorming session** – Discussions for the purposes of generating ideas and/or solving a particular problem.

**Bounded rationality** – The theory human minds are limited so decision-makers will satisfice rather than optimizing when making decisions.

**Capital asset pricing model** – A model using beta to calculate the required amount of return for an asset.

**Categorical imperative** – In Kantian moral philosophy, an obligation binding everyone at all times no matter what the circumstances are.

**Choice context** – The influence environmental factors have on decisions.

**Clear and convincing** – A legal standard greater than the preponderance of evidence (more likely than not) but lower than beyond a reasonable doubt.

**Coefficient of variation** – The expected value divided by the standard deviation.

61. Gladwell, M. (2005). **Blink:** The power of thinking without thinking. New York: Little, Brown and Co.

**Compensatory heuristic** – A decision-heuristic where negative or insufficient values attached to an attribute can be offset by higher values of another attribute.

**Complimentary events** – An event having only two outcomes: the event happened, or it did not happen.

**Compromise effect** – The tendency to avoid extreme options in decision making.

**Concave utility function** – A risk adverse utility function. This is the most common utility function. Most people are risk adverse.

**Conditional probability** – The probability of one event occurring given another has already occurred.

**Constrained optimization** – In economics, the optimization of profit or the minimization of cost given there are constraints on the decision- maker.

**Constraint function** – A mathematical condition the objective function must satisfy.

**Conventional wisdom** – The predictable and accepted choice when making a decision. The term is often attributed to the economist John Kenneth Galbraith.

**Convex utility function** – The utility function of a risk-seeker.

**Corner solution** – An optimal solution in a linear programming problem.

**Correlations** – The connection(s) between different variables often demonstrated by the use of mathematical models.

**Cost of capital** – The required rate of return used as a discount rate in determining the feasibility of a project.

**Critical path analysis** – A method of determining the shortest possible time to complete a project by determining which subtasks lie on the critical path and their required completion dates.

**Critical thinking** – Objective analysis aimed at making an informed and presumably correct decision.

**D**ata analysis – The process of preparing and analyzing data for the purpose of providing useful information for decision-makers.

**Data mining** – The search for correlations in Big Data.

**Data visualization** – Presentation of data in easily comprehended graphs and charts.

**Decision** – The result of decision analysis and a decision process.

**Decision analysis** – A variety of tools that can be brought to bear in analyzing and making a decision.

**Decision framing** – The choice of words or structure describing or delimiting a problem or decision. It can influence the outcome of a decision.

**Decision rule** – A method to judge or rank different outcomes.

**Decision tree** – A method of analyzing a complex decision by examining the branching of various expected outcomes.

**Declining marginal utility** – The economic theory stating each incremental unit of gain or consumption will produce a smaller and smaller increase in utility.

**Decoy effect** – The impact an added third option has on a binary choice.

**Delphi method** – A structured group process where panelists produce a consensus opinion through an iterative process.

**Deontological ethics** – An ethical system where actions are judged right or wrong by certain rules rather than by the consequences of the action.

**Dependent events** – The outcome of an event affects the probability of  a second event occurring.

**Discount rate** – The interest rate used in NPV computations.

**Discrete outcome** – The opposite of a continuous outcome. A discrete outcome can only take on particular values such as an integer.

**Disjoint events** – Mutually exclusive events that can't happen at the same time.

**Dominate** – An option is said to dominate another if at least one of its attributes are superior to the other option and none of its attributes are inferior to those of the second option.

**Double entry mental accounting** – An extension of the theory of mental accounting coupling the pain of loss with the pleasure of gains.

**Double down** – A term originating from the card game of blackjack. Doubling down in a business context means becoming more tenacious about defending a risky or incorrect decision when criticized.

**Dynamic programming** – A mathematical optimization process that derives a solution by breaking down a complex problem into subparts and solving those first.

**E**conomic man – A hypothetical persons who possesses perfect information and makes rational decisions maximizing their utility function.

**Efficient frontier** – The set of optimal solutions. Any potential solution not on the efficient frontier is inefficient and can be dominated by solutions on the efficient frontier.

**Elimination by aspects** – A decision rule formulated by Amos Tversky when faced with a multi-attribute decision. The decision-maker begins with the most important attribute and will consider only those above that meet or exceed a certain cutoff. The decision-maker then moves to the second most important attribute. This process continues until a final choice if made.

**Endowment effect** – People place a psychological value on property and feel pain when they have to give it up, even in a fair trade.

**Expected monetary value** – The amount of money you expect to receive based on a particular decision. The computation of the EMV employs probabilities to weight various possible outcomes.

**Even Swaps** – The process of making tradeoffs sequentially eliminating objectives by making them irrelevant to the decision.

**F**ama, Eugene (b.1939) – Co-winner of the 2013 Nobel Prize for economics and critic of behavioral finance.

**Fixed costs** – Costs that do not vary with the level of production.

**FOMO** – The fear of "missing out." The apprehension caused by the fear of missing an opportunity. It often leads to adopting the **"conventional wisdom."**

**Framing effect** – Choices are influenced by the way questions and challenged are presented or framed. This could include different words, contexts, or perceptions of gain or loss.

**G**ame theory – The study of how interacting choices affect the decision of the players as the game progresses.

**Groupthink** – Decision making by a group that prizes unanimity and harmony. It often leads to dysfunctional decisions.

**H**alo effect – The overall impression about a particular choice allows us to "fill in the blanks" about particular attributes of the choice.

**Hermeneutical insight** – A theological term describing how interpretations of sacred texts often depend on the exegete's understanding of certain portions of the text. This is often referred to as the "Canon within the canon problem."

**Heuristic** – A quick decision method best applied to decisions with small risk and small return.

**I**ndependent events – The probability of one event occurring is not affected by the occurrence or non-occurrence of a second event. The notation frequently used to describe this is $P(A|B) = P(A)$.

**K**ahneman, David – Nobel Prize Laureate who developed the theory of System 1 and System 2 thinking. Author of the book Thinking fast and slow. He, along with Amos Tversky are considered the fathers of modern decision analysis and behavioral economics. Kahneman won the Nobel Prize for Economics in 2002.

**Knight, Frank (1885-1972)** – American economist who defined risk as subject to probability estimation and uncertainty that was not.

**L**aplace strategy – Assume all possible outcomes are likely until you have evidence otherwise.This is employed in the accounting for contingent liabilities.

**Lexicographic heuristic** – Decision making based on one key attribute such as price, quality, reliability etc. There may be a hierarchy of decision attributes if the values of the key attribute are the same.

**Likelihood** – In Bayesian statistics, it is the new information modifying the prior probability.

**Linkage** – Connecting various negotiating issues into one global solution.

**Loss aversion** – The tendency to be much more sensitive to loss than to an equivalent amount of gain.

**M**arginal cost – In economic theory, the incremental cost of an additional cost of a unit utilized.

**Marginal probability** – The probability of an event occurring regardless of the occurrence of another event.

**Marginal revenue (benefit)** – In economic theory, the incremental revenue or benefit of an additional unit sold or obtained.

**Marginal utility** – In economic theory, the incremental pleasure derived from possessing or consuming one additional unit.

**Marker** – An indicator of a possible outcome, but not definitively the cause of the outcome.

**Maximax** – The game theory strategy seeking to maximize the probability of the maximum possible result.

**Maximin** – A decision rule calling choosing the best of the potentially adverse outcomes. It ignores upside gains and is inherently a pessimistic strategy.

**McCauley duration** – The weighted average time until all of a bonds cash flow is paid. A shorter duration implies less risk to the bondholder.

**Mental accounting** – Richard Thaler's theory of how people evaluate outcomes. Mental accounting can influence decisions in unexpected ways.

**Minimax** – A game theory strategy that selects the option guaranteeing the minimum of the maximum possible costs.

**Mixed cost** – A cost having fixed and variable components.

**Mixed strategy** – In game theory, a player randomly chooses a move from two or more random possibilities.

**Monte Carlo simulation** – A technique describing the impact of risk and uncertainty by modeling the probability of different outcomes.

**More likely than not** – Another name for the preponderance of evidence standard.

**Mutually exclusive events** – The occurrence of one event precludes the occurrence of the other.

**N**oncompensatory decision rule – Each decision attribute has a minimum cutoff. Advantages in some attributes cannot make up for the deficiency in other attributes.

**Nonprogrammed decision** – A new, novel or unique situation requiring a decision. The decision-maker does not have standard operating procedures or previous policies to use in making the decision.

**Nonsytemic risk** – In financial theory, market risk that can be diversified away. A well-diversified portfolio will eliminate all nonsystemic risk.

**O**bjective – The goal or the movement toward a goal of the decision.

**Objective function** – The mathematical function the decision-maker seeks to optimize subject to any constraint functions.

**Opportunity costs** – The potential gain lost from other alternatives when one alternative is chosen by the decision-maker.

**Out of pocket cost** – A cost requiring the direct payment of money or incurring a liability. It doesn't include any opportunity cost.

**Outcome and events** – An outcome is the result of a model or decision. An event is a set of outcomes with a defined probability. Rolling a die has six outcomes. An example of an event is the probability of rolling a five or under.

**Overchoice effect** – Occurs when too many options, including many acceptable choices are presented to the decision-maker. The decision-maker can be overwhelmed with the choices.

**P**areto efficiency – A situation where one party cannot be made better off without another party being made worse off.

**Pascal's Wager** – A proto-game theory exercise centering on the existence of God.

**Phantom decoy** – An alternative to another option but not available to the decision-maker at the time of choice.

**Perfect information** – The decision-maker has full and complete information about all decision attributes and their own utility function.

**Posterior probability** – In Bayesian statistics, the new probability after additional information has been assimilated into the prior probability.

**Practically dominate** – A practically dominated option is one inferior in at least one attribute to another option, but superior in another. The options it is dominant in are not deemed to be of sufficient consequence to offset its inferiority in others.

**Prediction markets** – A gambling forum where the crowd can place bets on the probability of an event occurring.

**Premortem** – After a group decision is made but before it is finalized, the participants are told to assume the decision turned out poorly and they must describe why. It is a way to mitigate groupthink.

**Preponderance of Evidence** – A standard of proof requiring only a greater than fifty percent probability to arrive at a decision.

**Prior probability** – In Bayesian statistics, the base rate or the probability of an event occurring before any new data is taken into account.

**Probability –** How likely it is an event will occur. This is described by a number from 0 to 1, with zero representing impossibility of the event occurring, and 1 representing certainty the event will occur. **Classical probability** requires each event having the same probability of occurrence. Rolling a two on an unloaded die has a one in six chance of happening. **Relative frequency** is the number of times something happens divided by all of the outcomes.

**Probability distribution –** A function describing the probability of obtaining values a random variable can assume.

**Probable and estimable –** The financial accounting standard for recording a liability and making appropriate disclosures about a contingency.

**Programmed decision –** Routine and repetitive decision handled by a standard operational policy and or procedure.

**Pros and Cons –** Constructing a list of all the pros (positives) for a choice on one side and all the cons (negatives) in a decision. The danger is each pro or con should not be weighted the same.

**Prospect theory –** People are risk averse. They judge gains and losses from a relative starting point rather than absolutely. Potential losses are more sharply felt than potential gains in making decisions under uncertainty.

**R**easonably possible **–** In U. S. accounting, a probability of occurrence between remote and probable. A loss contingency having a reasonable possibility of occurring must be accrued in the financial statements.

**Reason based choice –** The theory decision-makers will make a decision and then find reasons to support the choice.

**Recognition heuristic** – The decision-maker will choose an option they recognize rather than one that is not recognized.

**Regression to the mean** – A first extreme sample result will be followed by a second sample result closer to the population mean or a first sample result close to the population mean will be followed by a more extreme second sample result.

**Regret avoidance** – Decision-makers tend to regret poor decisions more if they do not follow conventional wisdom.

**Remote probability** – The occurrence of an event is extremely unlikely. In U.S accounting a loss contingency considered remote does not require either a loss accrual or disclosure in the financial statements.

**Risk averse** – The natural inclination of humans when facing risk or uncertainty. They attempt to reduce that risk or uncertainty as much as possible.

**Risk versus uncertainty** – According to Frank Knight's definitions, risk can be measured with a probability distribution. Uncertainty cannot be.

**S**abermetrics – A term invented by Bill James. The Society for American Baseball Research developed new and inventive ways to analyze Major League baseball decisions based on statistical analysis. Some of the new statistical measures such as Wins Above Replacement are controversial.

**Satisficing** – The first acceptable option encountered by the decision-maker is accepted and the decision analysis ceases. Satisficing saves time for the decision-maker and it will produce an acceptable but not necessarily the optimal result.

**Scenario planning** – Identification of potential uncertainties and the planned responses to each of them.

**Semi-lexicographic heuristic** – Similar to the lexicographic decision model but more flexible. Similar values of the main attribute are considered a tie, and the next decision factor is then evaluated.

**Sensitivity analysis** – A process that tests the output of a decision model by varying its underlying assumptions (and outcomes) a number of times.

**Sharpe ratio** – Excess return (defined as the return on a stock or portfolio less the risk-free rate of return) divided by the standard deviation of the stock or portfolio price.

**Simulation** – The imitation of a system or process over a period of time to predict outcomes or verify the output of the system or process.

**SMART analysis** – Acronym for the Simple Multi-Attribute Rating Technique, a decision analysis methodology for making decisions when multiple aspects must be taken into account.

**Stakeholder** – A person or another entity having a vested interest in an organization or a particular decision.

**Subjective probability** – A personal opinion of the probability of an outcome.

**Swing weights** – Weighting system used to determine the importance of attributes in SMART.

**Symmetrical measures of risk** – Positive and negative variances from expected value contributes just as much to the measure of riskiness.

**System 1 and System 2** – A description of how the human brain makes decisions. System 1 handles many routine functions such as driving. System 2 must be engaged to solve more complex problems. Unfortunately, System 2 is resource intensive and not good at multi-tasking.

**Systemic risk** – In financial theory, market risk that cannot be diversified away.

**T**haler, Richard (b. 1945) – Economist who studied and coined the terms mental accounting and behavioral economics. He won the Nobel Prize in Economics in 2017.

**Tornado diagram** – A graphical demonstration of the change in a result by changes in variables. Its most common format is a bar chart.

**Transitivity** – A person who prefers option A to B, and B to C must prefer A to C.

**Tversky, Amos (1937-1996)** – With Daniel Kahneman, the founder of prospect theory and major figure in advancing decision science.

**U**ncertainty versus risk – Risk can be quantified. Uncertainty can't. Uncertainty is not controllable, but risk can be.

**Utility function** – A model demonstrating a decision-maker's preference for certain alternatives based on satisfaction.

**V**ariable costs – Costs that vary by level of production.

**W**eighted Attribute Decision Models (WADM) – A decision methodology that uses weighting to determine the determine the importance of each decision factor. SMART is an example of WADM.

# Bibliography

Asimov, I. (1961). *The Machine That Won The War*. Mercury Press.

Asinof, E. (1963). Eight Men Out: The Black Sox and the 1919 World Series. Evanston, Ill: Holtzman Press.

Crumbley, D.L. Fenton Jr. , E.D., Zeigenfuss, D.E. (2014). *The Big R Foresnsic Accounting Adventure*. Durham N.C: Carolina Academic Press.

Dick, Philip K. (2002) *Minority Report*. London: Gollancz.

Gladwell, M. (2005). *blink*: The power of thinking without thinking. New York: Little, Brown and Co.

George, B., VUCA 2.0: A Strategy for Steady Leadership in an Unsteady World, Forbes Magazine, published 17 February 2017, accessed May 3, 2020.

Kahneman, D. (2011). *Thinking Fast and Slow*. New York: Farrar, Straus and Giroux.

Kahneman, D. and A. Tversky. "Subjective Probability: A Judgement of Representativeness." Cognitive Psychology 3 (1972).

Kahneman, D. and A. Tversky. "On the Psychology of Prediction." Psychology Review 80 (1973).

Knight, F. H. (1948). *Risk, Uncertainty, and Profit*. Boston: Houghton Mifflin Co.

Lewis, M. (2003). *Moneyball*: The art of winning an unfair game. New York: W.W. Norton.

Malmendier, U. and Tate, G. (2008). *Who Makes Decisions? CEO Overconfidence and the Market's Reaction*. Journal of Financial Economics. 89 July 2008.

Nassim Nicholas Taleb. (2016). Antifragile: Things that Gain from Disorder. Random House.

Nassim Nicholas Taleb. (2007). The Black Swan: The Impact of the Highly Improbable. Random House.

Ramos, M. "Auditors' Responsibility for Fraud Detection" Journal of Accountancy (January 2003).

Spielberg, S., Molen, G. R., Curtis, B., Parkes, W. F., Bont, J., Frank, S., Cohen, J., ... Twentieth Century-Fox Film Corporation. (2003). Minority report.

Surowiecki, J. (2005) The Wisdom of the Crowds. Anchor.

NOTES

Made in the USA
Middletown, DE
17 August 2021